NATIVE
HAWAIIAN
PLANTS

HOW TO GROW, CULTIVATE, AND ENJOY
25 POPULAR PLANTS

Kerin E. Lilleeng

Melany H. Chapin, Consulting Editor

MUTUAL PUBLISHING

I dedicate this book to:

The spirit of Mother Nature, for all of her magical creations,
and to those who strive to preserve them.

— Kerin E. Lilleeng

This is a condensed version of *Growing Hawai'i's Native Plants*
Copyright © 2018 by Mutual Publishing

ISBN-13: 978-1939487-96-4
Library of Congress Control Number: 2018948990

First Printing, October 2018
Second Printing, November 2022

Mutual Publishing, LLC
1215 Center Street, Suite 210
Honolulu, Hawaii 96816
Ph: (808) 732-1709
Fax: (808) 734-4094
e-mail: info@mutualpublishing.com
www.mutualpublishing.com

Printed in South Korea

Contents

Koa seedling — KL

Introduction

In view of the many requests for a condensed edition of *Growing Hawai'i's Native Plants,* this edition features twenty-five of Hawai'i's most widely-used native plants for the home garden.

WHAT ARE ENDEMIC HAWAIIAN PLANTS, AND HOW DID THEY GET HERE?

The Hawaiian Archipelago, nearly 2,500 miles from its nearest neighbor, is the most isolated landmass in the world. Unlike many other islands and island chains, which drifted away from their respective continents, geologic evidence indicates that the Hawaiian Archipelago is the result of volcanic activity be-

Wind dispersed seeds — KL

neath the seafloor, and has never been connected to any other land mass. So how did Hawai'i's unique flora and fauna arrive, and how did they become so well adapted to these isolated islands of lava?

WIND

Since the islands arose from the sea six million years ago, seeds and spores have arrived regularly. Many seeds, spores, and pollens are tiny and dust-like, and can drift airborne in the jet stream for exceptionally long distances. Surviving the freezing temperatures of the high jet stream, ferns, lichens, mosses, 1.4 percent of the flowering plants arrived in this fashion. An example is the ōhi'a lehua *(Metrosideros polymorpha),* which is a pioneer species, usually the first to become established on new lava flows along with ferns. Ōhi'a lehua seeds are still dispersed in this way and, unfortunately, so are many of the exotic plants that have more recently become naturalized and weedy in Hawai'i.

WATER

Of Hawai'i's native plants, 22.8 percent arrived floating in ocean currents. For this rare event to be possible, the seeds or plant parts must be able to float for long distances in seawater without germinating or losing their viability. Beach plants are the best example of this special adaptation of buoyancy:

some of the fruits contain corky materials or trapped air, while others have small coarse hairs on their seed coats called tomentose (for example, *Gossypium tomentosum*), allowing them to float. It is also believed that plants with individual seeds that could not float arrived by a process called rafting, in which great storms or other events uproot the entire plant, which then drifts in large vegetative mats to a new home. Some insects and small animals may have also arrived on rafting plants.

Wiliwili, beach naupaka and Kā'e'e seeds (wave dispersed) — KL

WING

Birds, responsible for bringing 74.8 percent of Hawai'i's endemic flowering plants to the islands, are the vehicles for the most incredible feat of seed dispersal: arrival on the wing. The seeds may have been stuck in mud on their feet, small barbed or sticky seeds may have attached to their bodies, or seeds may have been carried in their stomachs and excreted on arrival. Many of the small, seeded, wet-forest plants, whose fruit textures are still attractive to Hawai'i's native birds, were brought to Hawai'i by the ancestors to these birds.

Once the seeds arrived in the Hawaiian Islands, by wind, water, or wing, their biggest challenge still awaited them: growth and self-regeneration.

Many plants did adapt, evolving from somewhat small numbers of original immigrants, in isolated niches, and with very limited genetic material. In fact, it is thought that the 1,175 known flowering plants endemic to Hawai'i evolved from 272 original colonists (Wagner, W. L., et al. 2012). These new species coevolved in elegant equilibrium, losing chemical and mechanical defenses against grazing insects and animals that did not exist in the new environment. Instead they developed symbiotic relationships dependant on new species for food, pollination, and seed dispersal.

Recent fossil evidence indicates that the native lowland species stopped claiming new territory after

Native Koloa ducks (wing dispersed) — KL

Kaua'i's native blind cave wolf spider — KL

human contact, around 400 AD (Burney et al. 2001), a fact often attributed to the introduction of the rat and eventually, other grazing animals. Since the arrival of humans to the islands, 15,000–20,000+ and counting new plants have been introduced, along with numerous insects (increasing 20–30 percent per year) and animals. Many of these exotic plants, insects, and animals are so aggressive that Hawai'i's endemic species are losing the battle, becoming endangered or even extinct as they fail to produce seedlings and die out. Plants and seeds are being eaten by insects, rats, goats, and deer; pigs destroy seedlings while digging for food. Habitat destruction by humans and animals alike is on an enormous scale; its impact on the native plants has been devastating and almost incalculable.

Fortunately, landscapers, home gardeners, and public educators in Hawai'i have recently begun to take an interest in Hawai'i's priceless biological heritage. Hawai'i's children and adults are learning more about these plants and their amazing and unlikely journey. Almost 95 percent of native Hawaiian plants and animals occur nowhere else in the world, and Hawai'i's long isolation has meant that even today it has the highest percentage of endemics (90 percent endemic flowering plants) in the world per square mile of landmass. These facts alone should justify a great respect for these unique treasures of the Hawaiian Archipelago.

By writing this book and sharing over two decades of experience growing native Hawaiian plants, I hope to simplify the subject and make it enjoyable. My reward will be to see these beautiful plants, well adapted to Hawai'i's weather and soil, thriving in gardens, towns, and schoolyards across the state. What could be a better plant for our landscaping projects than one that has spent hundreds of thousands of years evolving in Hawai'i?

Wild goats Kōke'e, Kaua'i — KL

Seed Preparation

Native Hawaiian seeds — KL

Of the more than 310,000 flowering plant species in the world (Prance et al. 2000), 1,175 are native to Hawai'i (Wagner et al. 2012). There are more than thirty different types of native fruits and an equally diverse assortment of seed forms. The pericarp, or outer covering of the fruit, is the mature ovary and consists of the outer layer (epicarp), middle layer (mesocarp), and inner layer (endocarp). The seed is the mature ovule, and is made up of the seed coat (testa), enclosing the endosperm — the food for the new seedling — and the embryo, which eventually becomes the seedling. Fruits take diverse forms to utilize successful strategies to disperse or travel, or in some cases to stay close to the parent (Carlquist 1980). Fruits also have mechanisms to protect the embryo within the seed from animal digestion, and methods to cope with varying seasonal changes in rainfall and periods of drought. Some are even effectively scarified and dispersed by passing through the digestive tract of a bird. This extensive diversity in fruit and seed structures requires different methods of collecting, cleaning, storage, and treatments for successful germination. Following are general guidelines for the various kinds of fruits and seeds you will encounter.

Collecting Seeds

Fruit collection is one of the most important aspects of successful seed germination. If seeds are gathered when their embryos are insufficiently developed (immature), germination is greatly impaired. The seed is prone to be thin, light in weight, shriveled, poor in quality, and short-lived, producing a weak seedling or none at all. Ideally, seeds should be gathered from healthy, vigorous plants that are not stressed by drought or other unfavorable climatic conditions that might impair viability and/or increase disease before and during harvest. At

Abutilon menziesii x A. eremitopetalum hybrid — KL

the National Tropical Botanical Garden (NTBG) nursery, I grew native Hawaiian plants from all of the major islands in close proximity to each other. Often, these plants would cross-pollinate freely and would readily produce seeds. I tried to grow many of these crossbred seeds to see if they were viable or not, and they sometimes produced hybrid species. The *Abutilon, Bidens, Tetramalopium,* and *Schiedea* are some of the genera that produced hybrids within one generation. I have a beautiful cross between *Abutilon menzie-*

Alphitonia ponderosa seeds shriveled, insufficiently developed — DR

sii and *Abutilon eremitopetalum*. The plant has characteristics of both parents, and seeds produced by the hybrid stay true to the hybrid and do not revert back to either of the original parent species. To ensure a pure strain of seeds, collect them from the wild or from a controlled, pollinated plant, or use a clone (see page 22: Clonal Propagation).

Pulpy seeds — KL

FLESHY OR PULPY FRUITS

Collect fruits when they are as ripe as possible. Pulpy or fleshy fruits usually become soft when ripe and may change in color from green to white, black, orange, red, yellow, or other colors, depending on the species. Ripe fruits are easier to remove from plants, and will often fall off into your hands. Use plastic bags to help keep the pulp soft for easy removal until cleaning. If fleshy pulp is allowed to dry around the seed, it may create a very hard covering that will inhibit germination, as I have found to be true with sandalwood seeds.

DRY FRUITS (SEEDS)

Dry fruits have no pulp and are definitely dry at maturity (such as achenes, pods, and capsules). Try to collect these fruits on a dry day and keep them in a dry paper bag. Moisture can cause dry fruits to mold or rot and lose their viability. For these types of fruits, the drier the seed coat, the easier they are to clean.

Dry fruits — DR

KEEPING RECORDS AND LABELING

It is important to keep track of what you have collected, when it was collected, where, and by whom. This information can be important later to those who have questions and may want to contact you.

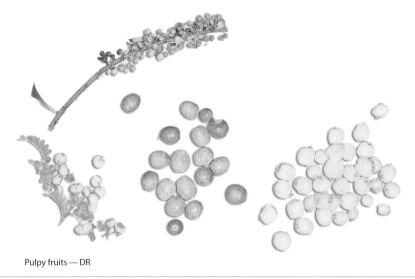

Pulpy fruits — DR

Keeping records and labeling — KL

Label your seeds, cuttings, air layers, and grafts with their species name, what treatments were used or not used, along with collection dates, date started, date germinated, what island they came from, and any other relevant information. If the information is not written down and attached to the plant, three months later when your seeds or cuttings have rooted, you will have forgotten all of the details and will lose valuable information. Popsicle sticks or any other water-resistant material that will take a mark are ideal. A dark pencil works best; it is long lasting, resists chemicals, and the sun will not fade the writing. Use your imagination and try other materials.

Cleaning Seeds

Cleaning seeds — DR

A fruit includes the seed(s) and the coverings, which can protect, disperse, and also inhibit germination of the seed(s) it envelops. The pericarp (fruit outer layer, middle layer, and endocarp) encase the seed(s). Although fruits are very diverse, the pericarp must be cleaned away before sowing or storage. Remove the surrounding pulp, capsules, pods, or other encasings, which can harbor strong germination inhibitors. They can also hold insects that will damage the seeds. Cleaning the pericarp away can help prevent the seeds from becoming spoiled, eaten, or diseased.

FLESHY OR PULPY FRUITS

If the pulp is allowed to dry around the seed, the resulting hard seed covering is likely to increase the seed dormancy and inhibit germination.

Large to medium seeds: To clean large to medium size fleshy seeds such as *Wikstroemia* or *Osteomeles,* first soak the seeds for an hour in a bowl of water to soften the pulp, if it is not already soft. The number of seeds you want to clean will determine the size of the bowl. Massage the fruits by hand, separating the pulp from the seeds. Pour off the floating pulp, then add more water and repeat this process until all of the pulp is gone. The heavier (viable) seeds will sink to the bottom of the bowl. The floating (non-viable) seeds can be poured off at the same time. Remember that some viable seeds will float at first, and then sink after a period of time (one to six hours). Seeds with corky or fuzzy coats will naturally float, since flotation in water is their dispersal mechanism. Most of these species are beach plants, such as *Myoporum,* but they will still benefit from being soaked.

Bug damaged seeds — KL

Manually cleaned seeds — KL

Small seeds: Small pulpy fruits are mostly from wet-forest plants that may have been carried to the Hawaiian Archipelago by birds, within mud on their feet, or in their stomachs. Use a strainer with a bowl of water. First, place the fruits in the strainer and put the strainer in the bowl of water. Rub the fruits against the strainer. This dislodges the seeds. The tiny seeds will fall through the strainer holes and into the bottom of the bowl. Pour off any floating pulp. Place a paper towel in the pulp-free strainer and pour the remaining water (with seeds) into the paper towel. Many alternative methods to the strainer and bowl exist, such as using an electric mixer or a blender with rubber blades, but the method given here is the simplest and works well without electricity. Let the seeds air-dry for a day before sowing. This will cut down on diseases that may reduce the effectiveness of germination.

DRY FRUITS (SEEDS)
Seeds that are from dry, dehiscent fruits such as grasses, follicles, capsules, and pods also have pericarps (seed coverings) that are dry at maturity. After collecting dry fruits, keep them dry. Leave them out at room temperature to air-dry, or in a dry paper bag. For smaller fruits, cleaning methods are the same as for small pulpy fruits except there is no water involved in the process. Be sure to choose a strainer that matches the seed size. Place the dry fruits into the strainer, then set the strainer into a bowl and carefully rub the fruits so that the seeds are dislodged and fall through the strainer into the bowl. This method is useful for small seeds in papery capsules such as *Dodonaea*.

CLEANING SEEDS MANUALLY
It is easier to manually remove large seeds in capsules or pods. Tools (for example, nail-clippers, a pocketknife, a hammer) and other implements can come in handy. Be very careful to avoid damaging the embryos. When you have collected and cleaned your seeds, they are ready for sowing or storage.

Storing Seeds

Seeds must be cleaned before storage. This includes the removal of any pulp, capsule, or other encasings, followed by air-drying. Germination inhibitors can be present in the pericarp, and seed-eating insects may be hiding in the capsule. Low moisture content in seeds during storage is the most important condition to maintain and monitor. Do not store seeds in plastic bags. Instead, I use sealed envelopes kept dry in storage containers in the refrigerator.

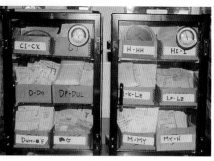

Seed desiccation chamber — DR

The NTBG conducted germination tests on the viability of seeds stored between one and eight years in desiccation chambers, using silica gel to maintain a relative humidity of 25% at room temperature. The results were interesting. In general, seeds that

Seeds storage in refrigerator — KL

occurred naturally in dry environments with dry seed coverings demonstrated high viability percentages after being stored in desiccation, whereas seeds from naturally moist environments, with fruity pulp coverings and softer seed coats, had very low viability or lost all viability after desiccation and storage.

DESICCATION

If seeds can tolerate desiccation without losing their viability, place them with the desiccant in an airtight container, storing in a cool, dry place. Try to maintain a relative humidity of 25%. Some seeds germinate even better after desiccation such as *Bidens* and *Eragrostis*.

TEMPERATURE

Seeds with hard seed coats in the legume family *(Fabaceae)* have high viability when stored in airtight containers without desiccants. They can be stored in the refrigerator or at room temperature in a dark, dry place. It is still important to keep out moisture so they will not germinate or rot.

Maile, loulu, and 'ōhi'a, short-lived seeds — KL

SHORT-LIVED SEEDS

Some seeds from wet-forest areas are meant to germinate right away and are short-lived. Often the very small seeds with only a soft seed coat or larger seeds like the native palm (Pritchardia), have no protective, hard seed coat and no dormancy capabilities. They will not tolerate storage and need to be sown immediately after cleaning. Otherwise they will quickly lose their viability.

The requirements for seed storage of the Hawaiian endemic species are not yet fully understood and need further research.

Methods of Propagation

Most books on propagation apply only to temperate zones and discuss such topics as double dormant embryos, winter callusing, stratification, heating pads, and enclosed glass greenhouses with elaborate heating and cooling systems. They include the basic methods on growing just about any plant that you desire, and all of this information can be found in any reliable propagation book. However, these procedures are not usually applicable when growing tropical plants in a tropical region. The growing seasons in Hawai'i are not limited, and freezing temperatures are not a consideration.

I have propagated and grew over 821 of the 1,386 species native to the Hawaiian Islands, from the common species to some of the most endangered plants in the world. More than once, I worked with only one seed or cutting from the last plant known to exist in the wild. These are nature's children, and they need extra protection in order to grow up healthy and strong — but anything special is worth a little extra time and effort. That is how I treat these plants, and it may be a contributing factor to the success I have in growing these unique and threatened keiki o ka 'āina (children of the land). The methods provided here are proven to work and are necessary in order to propagate and grow some of the more threatened plants native to Hawai'i.

NTBG collectors brought in material from all of the main islands; the material was immediately given a unique accession number, which links the plant to its collector, date, and origin. Since I received so many different kinds of seeds and other materials in large batches, I began to notice that in general the seeds from the same family behaved similarly (for example: drupes, pulpy or dry seeds, or pods) and needed to be cleaned, pretreated and sown in similar ways. This was also true to the generic level.

I have not had success with every species I have received. Some of the native plants that occur in small non-viable inbreeding populations are incapable of regeneration, and the seeds and cuttings failed to germinate or root. These plants need more work done on them; micro-propagation may be their only hope. Some plants may have a mycorrhizal fungi dependency. These plants need a particular fungus to survive and for their propagation. Mycorrhizal fungi exist in healthy soil and have a symbiotic relationship with roots of certain plants, such as native Orchids (Auge 1988).

Pretreatment of Seeds

Cleaned native seeds — KL

There are three factors in the successful germination of seeds. These are (1) seed viability, (2) removal of barriers to dormancy, and (3) fulfillment of the environmental needs of the seed. First, the seeds must be viable, with live embryos that are capable of germination. The collection of mature, ripe seeds from healthy plants that are not drought-stressed or stressed in any way will help ensure healthy embryos with sufficient amounts of stored food, capable of germination.

Second, seeds must be non-dormant, with no dormancy-inducing barriers present, whether they be physiological, physical, or chemical. Pulpy fruit and some thick seed coverings contain or create these barriers—hence the importance of cleaning seeds before sowing. If the seeds are dormant, the dormancy can be broken by various treatments described below. Third, seeds will not germinate or grow unless the environmental conditions normally required for growth are present. These include the proper moisture, temperatures, oxygen supply, and light levels. Seeds have strong survival tendencies and will not germinate unless these needs are met. In a controlled nursery setting, these environmental conditions can be created.

Soaking seeds — KL

PREGERMINATION TREATMENTS

Pregermination treatments help the seeds overcome any dormancy-inducing characteristics in the seed coat, and stimulate faster germination. Tropical plants, which have evolved in a warm climate, have different germination requirements than temperate plants. Generally speaking, native Hawaiian seeds do not require treatments that are often practiced in the temperate zones. For example, in temperate areas, stratification, which is a period of seed chilling, is often required for seeds that are accustomed to freezing winter soils. Similarly, the use of heating pads to help promote germination by keeping the seed mix warm is standard practice in colder regions but is not normally necessary for native Hawaiian plants.

Drupes have stone-hard endocarps (seed coat coverings) and are the most difficult seeds of the Hawaiian species to grow. These hard seeds need to be penetrated with water in order for the drupe to crack open along the seam for germination, like a peach seed does.

These are a few of the most troublesome genera in which to break dormancy. More research needs to be done to unlock their secrets. It is possible that they need a period of stratification, or require the presence of certain microorganisms in the soil.

I find that a combination of soaking seeds in water and scarification is the most effective treatment for the majority of native Hawaiian seeds. If you have an abundance of large seeds with thin, hard seed coats to treat, water soaking is easier and less time-consuming then scarifying each individual seed. For small numbers of large seeds, scarification works best, and results in a more uniform germination in a shorter period of time.

NOTE: Do not scarify a seed before soaking it in water.

When a seed is scarified and then soaked, it will quickly take up too much water, and the embryo will drown and rot instead of germinate. It is better to water soak to soften the hard seed coat first, and then scarify the seed. This will ensure a faster and more uniform germination.

WATER SOAKING

Water soaking is used to leach out any germination inhibitors in the hard, thick seed coats and to reduce the germination time. It is best to use twice as much water as there are seeds; the thicker the seed coat the longer the soaking time. Change the water daily or when needed. Water is absorbed rapidly by the dry seeds at first, then the rate of absorption levels off. The seed swells, and the seed coat may break open. This is an excellent indicator that the seed is ready for germination, and the water soaking should end promptly. Be careful that excess water does not become trapped between the cotyledons (seed leaves), which can suffocate the embryo. Take out the swollen seeds and continue soaking the remaining seeds until they undergo a similar change. Each genus has specific soaking times and treatments within the family profiles.

Hand-hot or tap water: Hand-hot or tap water can be used. Hot water at 120–135°F (50–57°C) is recommended for harder, thicker seed coats. If the water is too hot for your hand, it is too hot for the seed. Cool tap water is fine for most species. At first, some seeds will float; stir them around to dislodge any trapped air pockets. After soaking for twelve hours or so, the viable seeds will sink to the bottom, while the non-viable seeds tend to float. If a seed floats, the embryo is probably dead, and there may be air pockets where the live embryo should be. Discard the non-viable seeds by pouring them out. Remember that not all seeds will sink. Some are meant to float; that is how many of them originally arrived in the Hawaiian Islands.

Soaking times: Soaking times vary from a few minutes to a few days, depending on the seed type. Place the viable, pretreated seeds on a paper towel to dry for storage, or sow right away.

SCARIFICATION

Scarification is the method of creating a crack or opening in the seed coat to allow the absorption of water and gases for germination. A few examples of nature's scarification methods include cracks created in hard, thick seed coats by rolling over rocks in streambeds, microorganism activity in the soil, or passage through an animal's digestive tract. Water soaking does not work for all types of seeds; in some cases seed coats are so thick and tough that the absorption of

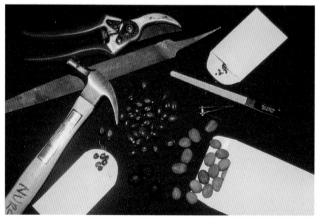

Tools to scarify seeds — DR

water or oxygen is prevented, and they are dormant. The dormancy in such seeds may sometimes be broken artificially by scarification. One example is *Acacia koa*.

If you are working with small numbers of large seeds, any of these methods is effective:

Scarifying wiliwili seeds — DR

- Rub a small area of the seed coat with sandpaper or a file to expose the embryo;
- Nick the seed coat with clippers, pruners, or hand shears to create a hole in the hard seed coat, avoiding the embryo (this is my preferred method);
- Gently crack the seed coat with a small hammer along the seam of the seed making sure not to smash the seed.
-

If you are working with large numbers of seeds with hard seed coats, this method is effective:

- Use a stone polisher, tumbler, or concrete mixer with fine cinder or sand of a different size than the seeds to promote adequate scarification;
- Check the seeds periodically to ensure that the inner parts of the seed are not overexposed, which can damage the delicate embryos;
- If you leave the seeds in the mixer too long, you will remove too much of the seed coat.

ACID SCARIFICATION

Some horticulturalists use acid scarification to break down hard or impermeable seed coats (sandalwood). This treatment was not included in this study and consequently no results were obtained. It did not seem necessary here, and I feel this method is not entirely safe to work with.

NO PRETREATMENT

Very small seeds usually have thin seed coats and very little endosperm, and consequently have no dormancy period and do not require any pretreatment. However, it is important to remove all the fleshy pulp from these seeds and

'Ōhi'a seed capsules and seeds (no pretreatments) — KL

sow them soon after cleaning. These types of seed do not store well. Two examples are *Brighamia* and *Metrosideros.*

There are many ways to clean, treat, and sow seeds. The methods described here are simple and have proved successful for me. They have been effective in growing all the different seed types from the various distinct habitats in which the native plants evolved. Do what works best for you in your growing environment. The important thing is to enjoy the process of growing native Hawaiian plants.

Germination

'A'ali'i seedlings — KL

The majority of native Hawaiian seeds take one to six months for of all the viable seeds to germinate. You will usually have to wait until the seedlings have between two and six true leaves before transplanting. Some seedlings need a little help getting their first leaves out of the seed coats. If within two to three days after they germinate their seed coats are still attached to the cotyledons, you may need to help by carefully and slowly peeling off the seed coat. When only a few of the seeds have sprouted out of a flat, transplant them and keep the flat intact for two more months. Others may germinate later; this is usually the case. Even some pretreated seeds will take up to a year to sprout. If you can, keep seed flats for a full year, which gives all of the seeds the opportunity to sprout.

You have collected mature, ripe seeds, and cleaned and pretreated them to hasten germination. Now it is time for the fun part: growing the seeds! It is always best to start your seeds in the spring and summer months, with longer days and more sunlight. I have observed that some species of seeds will wait until spring to germinate, even though they were sown in the late fall.

The process of seed germination involves four factors:
- Moisture absorption (affects both germination percentage and the rate);
- Favorable soil temperatures (required to change stored foods into usable sugars);

- Oxygen (stimulates the embryo cells to grow);
- Light (promotes germination in most species and affects soil temperatures).
- Adding a small amount of healthy native soil that they were growing in, to the sterile mix, for mycorrhizal fungi dependent plants. I feel most rare native plants difficult to grow in cultivation have a MF dependence.

The growing embryo then swells, splitting the seed coat as it germinates.

SEED POTTING MIXES

A good germination mix should supply seeds with the proper moisture, soil temperature, and oxygen. Most importantly, the mix should allow for excellent drainage and aeration. This reduces surface crusting caused by algae growth and discourages damping-off (for example, if fungi are allowed to spread, it can cause seedling death). The mix should also have a neutral pH (6.5–7.0) and be free of any weed seeds, insects, herbicides, pesticides, or diseases. Try to buy potting mixes especially made for growing seeds; avoid mixes with compost, shredded bark, sawdust, or wood shavings that may not be fully decomposed and could contain resins or tannins; these materials can be toxic to immature seedlings. Buying non-soil mixes that are pasteurized with steam will help control some of these problems. These mixes are made up of sphagnum peat moss (55 percent – 65 percent), perlite, dolomite limestone as a pH adjustment, and gypsum, a wetting agent. Initial seed germination will occur without any immediate nutrition, since the seed lives off stored foods in the seed endosperm. Even when I had this basic knowledge about potting mixes, I still did not know the best mix to use for growing native Hawaiian plants from all of the different plant communities. The soils and environments are so different from those on the mainland, were these mixes are made. I set up experiments with different mixtures, watering times, and recorded the results. One thing is certain: native plants are very sensitive to poor soil drainage. This unquestionably causes damping-off and/or surface crusting. This can be easily solved, either by adding extra perlite or clean-rinsed cinder to the mix to promote drainage, or by reducing the frequency of watering.

RECOMMENDED SEED MIX

Combinations of materials give better aeration and results than a single mix used alone. No fertilizer should be added to the media for seed mixtures. Sunshine Mix No. 4® is my preferred potting mix. These mixes can be used:

- 2 or 3 parts perlite to 1 part potting mix (3:1);
- 2 or 3 parts perlite to 1 part coarse vermiculite (3:1) (good for beach plants);
- 2 or 3 parts small rinsed cinders to 1 part potting mix (3:1).

Your decision about whether to add more perlite to the potting mix will depend on the amount of moisture in the air. The wetter the environment, the more perlite or cinder should be added to the mix. This is important for areas with timed mist systems. For drier environments, you need more potting mix or vermiculite to retain more moisture. Do not mix vermiculite and potting mix together; they both hold water and will pack together in a flat, reducing the airflow through the mix and causing damping-off problems. Uniform moisture to the upper layers of the potting mix is essential, yet excessive moisture will cause diseases. An excellent solution is to place the seed flats on a controlled mist bench with a timer. For those of us who do not have access to mist benches, watering every other day with a misting nozzle attached to a watering can or garden hose is sufficient.

CONTAINERS

Flats — shallow plastic, wooden, or metal trays 3–4 inches deep — are used for germinating seeds or rooting cuttings. I like to recycle containers that we normally throw away, like tofu or mushroom trays or foil cake pans. They are the perfect size and depth for seedlings; all you need to do to these everyday containers is add the proper drainage holes. Make sure that the drainage holes are made from the inside out, and that your containers are cleaned thoroughly to avoid contamination. Fill your shallow container to ¼ inch from the brim with a well-drained mix; pat down the corners and edges evenly.

SOWING SEEDS

Planting the seed at the proper depth is a critical factor. If the seed is planted too shallow, the seed may dry out too quickly. If the seed is planted too deep, seedling emergence will be delayed. The size and the kind of seed being sown determines the proper depth. Keep the mix moist, but on the dry side, and water after sowing the seeds as this helps them settle to the right depth in the mix, according to their weight.

- Tiny seeds may be too small to break through a layer of germinating mix. Surface sowing on a well-drained potting mix easily solves this. In a dry mix, the seeds sink into the mix better. Use a fine mist to water the seeds in, so as not to blow the tiny seeds away. They will settle into the mix to the proper depth for their germination. One example is *Metrosideros*.

- Medium-sized seeds should be covered lightly with mix; the depth should be about the same as the diameter of the seed. The seed should not be visible after watering; if it can be seen, add a little more mix and water again. Examples include: *Wiksoemia* and *Osteomeles*.
- Large seeds that are fast-germinating may be planted in individual pots, at a depth that is two to three times their diameter. Most large seeds are fast-growing trees with long taproots. In this case use a deeper pot (e.g., a taproot pot) so the root has room to grow down. Germination is fast (about one week), especially after being pretreated.

WATER REGIMES

Aim for a constant, moderate degree of moisture during germination. The mix should not dry out or be soggy, both of which contribute to seedling death. Watering in the morning is recommended, ensuring that the mix will not be too moist during the night, as this can invite diseases. Any intermittent mist systems should be turned off at night, and turned on only during daylight hours, roughly between 6 a.m. to 6 p.m.

Water every other day unless your growing environment is very dry (such as Kahoʻolawe), in which case, water every day. Keep the seed containers up off the ground away from slugs, toads, and/or soil-borne diseases. Also, keep them under a covered, shaded area, protected from heavy rains, wind, and direct sunlight, which can be excessively hot and drying, until the seeds have germinated. Once they germinate, start to furnish additional light. For those that do not have access to a nursery, starting your seedlings under a shady tree is fine, but keep the falling leaves out of the seed containers, as they can cause problems with damping-off and can hide slugs, which love to eat seedlings.

ʻĀkia seedings — KL

Slugs are capable of eating an entire plant or flat of seedlings in one night; use bait to control the slugs.

SEEDLING CARE

Germination can vary from one week to two to three years, depending on the species, but for most seeds, one to three months is normal. Be patient, as growing these rare gems is not the same as growing vegetables. The first leaves which appear on many dicot seedlings are two seed leaves or dicotyledons, often bearing little to no resemblance to the later leaves, known as true leaves. For monocots, such as grasses, palms, and lilies, the monocotyledon, appearing as the seed itself is attached to the new

Potted seedlings of **Brighamia insignis** – NTBG nursery — DR

seedling, emerges as the first true leaf. All seedlings after germination need light to develop into strong, healthy plants. In dim light, they will grow elongated, with weak, spindly stems. Seedlings also need good air circulation, so avoid locations that are too closed-in, and do not overcrowd the plants on the benches. Monitor seedling stems carefully for signs of damping-off: the base of the stem will turn brown and collapse even though the leaves still look healthy. Damping-off is encouraged by soil that is too wet and poor ventilation. Reduce watering; a fungicidal drench may also help. Seedlings whose leaves droop and shrivel or whose stems bend over are probably too dry. In this case, water the flat thoroughly.

Feed seedlings before transplanting. When watering your seedling flats, simply use a weak liquid fertilizer solution (¼ tsp. to 1 gallon water). Your seedlings should be kept healthy, and have a strong green color until transplantation into their own pots. For some seedlings, such as those from tiny seeds, the time from germination to transplanting can be as long as six months or more. Examples include: *Metrosideros* and *Brighamia*.

TRANSPLANTING AND MEDIA
Transplanting
- For the best result, wait until the dicot seedling has two to four true leaves and monocot seedlings are 2 inches tall.
- If dry, water seedling flats one hour before transplanting. This reduces transplant shock.
- Half-fill pots with slightly moist soil mix.
- Gently remove seedlings from flat. Only handle the seedling by the leaves, or the soil ball around the roots. Do not handle the stem, which is very delicate and easily injured. Use your hand or finger to loosen and lift them from the flat; carefully pull them apart, trying not to disturb the small ball of roots and clinging mix.

- Place the root ball into the half-filled pot, then add the remaining soil, and cover the roots only to the base of the stem, not up to the leaves.
- Thoroughly water pots with a fine spray nozzle. Straighten out any seedlings lying down after watering.
- Label the pots with the plant name, date started, transplanted, etc.
- Keep them moist and out of direct sunlight for a week or so, then gradually move them from filtered sun to full sun in a couple of weeks, depending on the individual plant's needs.

Transplant mixes: A totally sterile mix is not necessary at this point; use some of the soil the plants will be living in.

Heavy soils, such as clay
2 to 3 parts perlite or cinder
1 part clay soil
1 part bagged potting mix

Medium soils, such as organic forest litter
3 parts perlite or cinder
1 part soil
1 part bagged potting mix.

Light soils, sandy loams
1 part bagged potting mix
1 part sandy soil
2 parts perlite or cinder (if sand is fine-textured)

Volcanic soils
1 part bagged potting mix
2 to 3 parts volcanic soil (cinder)

Compost soils
2 to 3 parts perlite or 2 parts cinder
1 part well-decayed compost soil
1 part bagged potting mix

The soil mixture you choose to make should depend on the location and environment the plants will be growing in. The wetter it is, the more drainage your mix will need.

NUTRITION AND FERTILIZERS

I have found that native plants are sensitive to strong fertilizers, and that half the recommended dosage is sufficient. Add the fertilizer when mixing the soil; do not add it on top of the mix.

I recommend using an organic, slow-release fertilizer of 8-8-8 NPK and micronutrients (minor elements), not present in sterile potting mixes and lacking in some of the depleted Hawaiian soils. These fertilizers provide nutrients to the plants gradually over a long period of time and reduce the possibility of fertilizer burn. Between once a month and once every three months, foliage-feed your potted plants with a liquid fertilizer (following directions on the label). The nozzle feeder works well for this.

Native Hibiscus from Kerin's yard — KL

Asexual (Clonal) Propagation

Unrooted to rooted *Hibiscus brackenridgei* cuttings — KL

CUTTINGS

Propagation of cuttings, the most widely used method of propagation, is a method of genetic cloning or asexual reproduction of the parent plant. Cuttings are taken from the vegetative portions of the plant: the leaves, stems, roots, and modified stems (tubers, rhizomes, corms, and bulbs).

The condition of the parent plant supplying the cuttings is very important. Generally speaking, the more vigorous and healthy the parent is, the better the cuttings will root and grow. My goal when starting cuttings is a 100 percent success rate. These are the steps I take to achieve this goal.

It is important to have clean, sharp tools for taking the cuttings. A sharp cut at the basal end ensures less damage to the cells that will be forming the roots, and clean tools help to prevent the spread of plant pathogens from plant to plant. If for some reason the cuttings cannot be started right away, keep them in a sealed plastic bag in the refrigerator no longer then a day or two. This helps keep them moist and turgid with an abundance of stored foods for rooting. The longer you wait to start the cutting the lower your rooting percentage will be.

For maximum results take cuttings in the cool morning hours to ensure the cuttings have a high level of stored foods (carbohydrates) to nourish the developing roots and leaves until the new plant becomes rooted and self-sustaining. The stored foods are carried from the top of the plant to the roots during the heat of the day. To regulate the plant's water levels, the plant transpires by using stomata, which are tiny pores opening in the epidermis (surface) of the leaves, which control moisture and gas exchange. Avoid collecting cuttings from plants that are infested with insects or are diseased or drought stressed. If drought is a problem, water the plant for a week before taking the cuttings to ensure a higher level of stored foods for growing healthier roots.

Stem cuttings are divided into four different types, depending on the stem maturity, the time of year the cuttings are taken, and the plant type. For Hawai'i, the best season to collect cuttings is from early spring to mid-summer. The four types of cuttings are hardwood, semi-hardwood, softwood, and herbaceous.

HARDWOOD

Hardwood cuttings are made from the mature wood of last year's growth from hardwood trees and shrubs. Cut brown woody stems of moderate size from the central or basal shoots (not from weak growing interior shoots).

The cuttings should be 1–4 inches in diameter, and 5–12 inches long with at least three nodes. The top cut should be ¼ – 1 inch above a node at a right angle; the basal (base) cut is made just below a node at a slant, exposing more rooting cells; the cutting size depends on the type of plant. Longer and thicker cuttings take longer to root, and are harder to handle when they are potted up.

At the time the hardwood cuttings are taken, remove all of the leaves, ensuring that the cuttings will retain more moisture and will root faster. If you choose to leave some foliage on, reduce it by cutting the foliage in half.

Remove all of the green tips from these cuttings to where the woody portion starts, as hardwood tip cuttings are lower in stored foods and root poorly. Also remove all the leaves remaining and any small side shoots since these leaves and shoots allow essential stored moisture to escape, take up more room in the rooting flat, and leaves would probably fall off eventually into the rooting mix increasing the likelihood of disease.

Start your collection of cuttings as soon as possible into a sterile cutting mix. It is important not to let the cuttings dry out or be exposed to the full sun at any time prior to rooting. Keep the cuttings in a clean, sealed plastic bag, wrapped with damp clean newspaper or sphagnum moss — anything that will keep them moist during transport. If you can, put the bag of cuttings in a cool ice chest with an ice pack during transport to the growing area, but make sure

Plumbago cuttings – NTBG nursery — KL

Herbaceous cuttings — KL

Nephrolepis cordifolia – tubers and rhizomes — KL

not to keep loose cuttings on loose ice cubes in the chest as this will damage them.

To prepare cuttings for rooting: just before starting, re-cut the base at a 45-degree angle, exposing fresh cells, then dip the freshly cut surface into the appropriate rooting powder. Insert the cuttings 3–4 inches apart into the rooting mix with at least one or two nodes under the mix. Make sure that the larger cuttings are securely held in place during rooting but are not planted so deep that the base of the cutting does not receive proper aeration (airflow), a requirement of healthy rooting.

SEMI-HARDWOOD

Semi-hardwood cuttings are those taken from trees and shrubs in the summer months from the new shoots, just after the flush of spring growth, when the wood is partially mature. Make the cuttings 3–7 inches long, with at least three nodes. Remove only the lower foliage and retain three or four new leaves on the top. Remove any bug-infested leaves to stop further damage. Semi-hardwood cuttings are more prone to drying out. To avoid this, follow the directions above for keeping cuttings moist during transport.

If the top leaves are more then 2 inches long, reduce the leaves in size by cutting them in half. This lowers the water loss and allows for closer spacing in the cutting flat.

Just before starting: re-cut the base at a 45-degree angle, then apply rooting powder. Place cuttings 2–3 inches apart, with one node inserted into the rooting mix.

Cuttings should be rooted under conditions that will minimize water loss from the leaves. Root under an intermittent mist system or in a covered cool moist place, off the ground, and out of the direct sun. Placing the pot of cuttings in a sealed plastic bag works well in drier locations to keep them moist, but be careful not to keep it too wet or the cuttings may rot.

SOFTWOOD

Softwood cuttings are taken from small shrubs and groundcovers whose stems are soft and succulent, or from the plant's new spring growth. Softwood cuttings should be 3–6 inches long with at least two or three nodes. Again, remove only the lower foliage and retain the top leaves. Cut the leaf in half if it is more then 2 inches long. Place cuttings 2 inches apart in shallow rooting flats, with at least one node inserted into the well-drained rooting mix.

These cuttings generally root more quickly and easily than any other type, but they require more constant attention to keep them from drying out completely at any time during rooting. If at all possible, place them under a controlled mist system for rooting, or in a covered, cool, moist, shaded place, away from the direct sun. Water them daily in the morning, or if they are in drier locations, place the pot of cuttings within a sealed plastic bag, out of direct sun.

HERBACEOUS

Herbaceous cuttings are from succulent plants that usually do not develop woody stems and stay succulent through out the year. Follow the directions for starting softwood cuttings.

Again, drying out is the biggest problem associated with rooting these cuttings, unless they are from very dry areas. These will need to dry out slightly for a few days to a week, similar to cactus or plumeria cuttings' need to callus before planting to avoid rotting.

Rooting hormones — KL

TUBERS OR RHIZOMES

The tuberous or rhizomatous stem of the native begonia *(Hillebrandia)* and some ferns can be divided after new growth starts in the spring. Make sure that every 3–5-inch section has at least one bud for new growth. Gently dig under the plant until you find the tuberous or rhizomatous root system; cut a section with buds 3–5 inches long. Keep these cuttings moist and in a plastic bag until planted into 2–3 parts black cinder or perlite to 1 part potting mix (3:1). Keep cuttings cool, moist, and out of direct sun.

ROOTING HORMONES

Rooting hormones are synthetic, root-promoting chemicals that stimulate root growth. The purpose of treating the basal ends of cuttings with hormones is to increase the rooting percentage and hasten rooting time. Both the powder and liquid forms are satisfactory. I prefer rooting powders as they are easier to work with, but be sure to carefully follow the directions on the label. Powder hormones with added fungicides are especially useful for wetter growing conditions. More details will be provided on specific hormones within the genus profiles.

- Hardwood cuttings use rooting powder Nos. 8–30 and up.
- Semi-hardwood cuttings use Nos. 3–8.
- Softwood cuttings use Nos. 1–3.
- For herbaceous cuttings, use No. 1 with fungicide or no rooting powders at all. They still root easily enough without added stimulants.

Cutting mix: The cutting mix has three functions:
- To hold or support the cutting in place during the rooting period;
- To permit proper aeration to the base of the cutting;
- To provide adequate moisture to the cutting.

There is no one ideal rooting medium. Instead, there are several different combinations of materials that will make a good workable mix that provides sufficient porosity to allow good aeration and has a high water-holding capacity that nevertheless drains well and is free from harmful diseases and weed seeds. The requirements are the same for germinating seeds.

Recommended cutting mixes

- 2–3 parts perlite to 1 part vermiculite
- 2–3 parts perlite to 1 part potting mix or 1 part coarse vermiculite
- 2–3 parts rinsed clean fine cinder to 1 part potting mix
- 100 percent rinsed-clean fine cinder will work, but it can dry out faster. It is, however, a good mix for use under an intermittent-mist system.
- Oasis cubes work well, but can be expensive.

A good basic mix uses a pasteurized, soil-less mix, to ensure that there are no weed seeds, pesticides, insects, or diseases to disrupt rooting. Avoid mixes with untreated ground pine bark, sawdust, or sand added; these mixes are not pasteurized, and diseases might be present. I do not suggest combining potting mix with vermiculite, because they both hold water and eventually restrict the proper airflow, which may rot the cuttings (unless you are in a very dry location with limited water). My preferred mix is Sunshine Mix No. 4®.

CONTAINERS AND WATERING

Smaller cuttings should be in shallow flats 3–6 inches deep, with drainage holes. These containers need to be deep enough to insert at least one node at the base of the cutting below the mix surface and hold the cutting firmly in place without movement during rooting. For larger cuttings a 3-gallon pot, half filled with rooting mix, works well.

WATERING CUTTINGS

Chlorinated tap water is preferable to lake or stream water, since tap water contains fewer living disease organisms, salts, or algae. These can accumulate in the cutting mix and reduce or even prevent rooting. Rainwater is best, if it is pure.

The cutting mix should be leveled and watered thoroughly with a fine spray nozzle before the cuttings are inserted. Afterwards, water lightly to settle the mix around the cuttings enough to help hold them in place, but not enough to wash away the rooting powder you have just applied to the base. For the cuttings that have foliage remaining and are not under a mist system, several light sprinklings with a fine mist of water each day is better than a heavy soaking less frequently. Never allow the mix to stay excessively wet or to dry out completely during rooting.

Cuttings will root with the proper moisture and hormone treatment anywhere from two weeks to six months after planting, sometimes longer, depending on the species and the time of the year the cuttings were taken. Rooting times will be specified within the family and genus profiles.

THE CARE OF CUTTINGS DURING ROOTING

Cuttings must be placed in a covered, shaded area, out of the direct sun and strong winds.

Remove all dropped leaves and sprouted weeds immediately from the flats, along with any obviously dead cuttings. This helps to prevent the spread of disease.

If mites, aphids, or mealy bugs appear on the cuttings, control promptly. They can be rubbed off by hand or, for large numbers of cuttings, sprayed with a mild insecticidal soap.

After your cuttings start to grow new foliage, fertilize them monthly with a foliar feeding fertilizer. Miracle Gro® works well, and is easy to use with a nozzle applicator.

TRANSPLANTING ROOTED CUTTINGS

A good indicator that the cuttings are rooted is a flush of new growth. When gently tugged, they should give resistance. Carefully dig under a cutting to check for a sizable root system. If you are patient and wait until they are well rooted, with a small, fibrous root ball, before transplanting them from the rooting mix, you will have a higher survival rate. Transplant during the cool morning hours. Rainy days are also good, or in shady conditions. However, do not expose new delicate roots to direct sun, or allow them to dry out during potting.

Choose a pot a little larger then the root ball; half-fill the pot with a well-drained soil (the same as for seedlings). Carefully and gently loosen the mix around the cuttings by moving your hand under the mix and root ball; do not pull or tug the cutting out, as this may damage the roots. Place the cutting in the pot, then cover the roots with remaining soil, and gently tap down to stabilize the cutting.

Water thoroughly. It is critical that the water drains freely, and does not sit on top of the soil mix. Keep the newly potted cuttings in a shaded area out of the wind for two to three weeks, and then move them into more sun to harden them off and prepare them for outplanting in six to twelve months, depending on the plant.

TRANSPLANT MIXES

At this point, a totally pasteurized, sterile mix is not necessary. It is more important that the mix is well-drained, to encourage healthy growth.

Heavy soils, such as clay
3 parts perlite or cinder
1 part soil

1 part bagged potting mix

Medium soils, such as organic forest litter
2–3 parts perlite or cinder
1 part soil
1 part bagged potting mix

Light soils, sandy loams
2–3 parts perlite or cinder
1 part bagged potting mix
1 part light soil

Volcanic cinder soils
1 part bagged potting mix
1 part volcanic cinder

Compost soil
3 parts perlite or cinder
1 part compost soil
1 part bagged potting mix

The soil mixture you choose should depend on the location and the environment the plants will be growing in. The wetter the environment, the more drainage the mix will need.

Soil drainage can be easily increased by amending the soil with perlite, medium cinder, or pumice. To help the soil hold more moisture, use potting mixes with peat moss, shredded sphagnum moss, and vermiculite.

NUTRITION AND FERTILIZERS

Native plants are very sensitive to strong fertilizers (14-14-14 and higher). Applications using half of the recommended dosage is sufficient. In this case, more is not always better; if you have any doubt use less.

I prefer to use an organic, slow-release fertilizer. These fertilizers provide nutrients to the plants gradually over a longer period, and help reduce the possibility of injury from excessive application. I recommend 8-8-8 NPK fertilizer, and micronutrients (minor elements) not present in sterile potting mixes and lacking in some of the depleted soils of Hawaiʻi. Add the fertilizer and micronutrients when mixing the soil, not on the surface afterwards.

Once a month, foliage feed your plants. A liquid fertilizer, using the nozzle applicator, is easy and it works well.

AIR LAYERING

Air layering is a form of asexual propagation by which a branch on a tree or shrub is made to root while still attached to the parent plant. This is one of my favorite methods of plant propagation. Air layering is used on plants that are not easily propagated from seeds or cuttings, or when a larger plant is desired in a shorter period of time. It is commonly used on tropical fruit trees such as lychee. Some native plants are so endangered that as a conservation measure, we air layer the large branches that need pruning instead of pruning and throwing them away.

Air layers on ma'o hau hele – KL

The great advantage to air layering is that your rooted air layer will act the same age as the parent plant it is taken from and will flower and fruit far sooner than a seedling or cutting. Of the native plants I have air layered, such as *Hibiscus,* and *Metrosideros,* all have rooted readily within three months. My experience suggests that most native Hawaiian plants are good candidates for air layering. However, more research needs to be conducted on air layering other native plants before this subject is clearly understood.

When air layering, it is always best to choose healthy, vigorous growing trees or shrubs that are in the ground, as opposed to containers. You may have more control over the progress and final results if you have the opportunity to use parent plants that are on private property. They can be monitored from time to time, whereas in the wild there is no guarantee that your air layers will still be there when you return in three months' time. On state or federal land, you will need to obtain the proper permits. Private property, of course, also requires permission from the owner. For unknown reasons, all of the air layers I started in the wild for NTBG were cut off and taken by other people before they could root properly.

In Hawai'i, air layering can be done at any time of the year as long as the bark of the plant is easily removed. The optimum time of year for this is the early spring months (March, April, May) just before the new growth begins. Roots will develop in two to six months.

Select a well-shaped, woody branch of the previous year's growth 1–6 inches in diameter. Remove any branches in your way to give your hands plenty of room to move around. Larger branches can be air layered, but rooting is less satisfactory and the resulting roots are usually not strong enough to hold up the larger plants.

Hibiscus brackenridgei rooted air layers — KL

With a clean, sharp knife make a girdle around the branch, making sure you go deep enough to completely remove a stripe of bark from the branch ½ to 1½ inches wide depending on size of the branch; if the bark does not slip (peel off), the plant is not in the proper phase of growth for air layering. There is no point in continuing unless the bark peels off freely.

Scrape the newly exposed, light-colored woody surface to ensure the complete removal of the cambium (cells that form new tissues). If the cambium layer is not removed, callus will grow over the girdled area, preventing root development.

Apply rooting powder to the top of the girdled area. When air layering a species for the first time, I use different hormone strengths to test which ones root the best. More specific hormone strengths will be discussed for each plant within the family and genus profiles.

Place about two handfuls of slightly damp sphagnum moss with all of the excess moisture squeezed out around the stem, enclosing the area that is girdled and covered with hormone; if the sphagnum moss is too moist, the girdled area will rot.

Wrap a piece of plastic wrap, 8–10 inches square, completely around the moss. Tie both ends securely with a waterproof material such as electrical or half-inch green garden tape, particularly the upper end, to prevent any additional moisture from entering during heavy rains.

Then wrap aluminum foil 8–10 inches square, dull side up, around the entire air layer, tightly tying both ends. This provides darkness for the newly forming roots and creates a more uniform root ball, as the roots tend to avoid the sun. It also helps protect the plastic wrap from the elements.

Remember to always keep records of the rooting powder used, the date the air layer was made, etc., so you will know what works or does not work.

Rooting takes two to six months, depending on the kind of plant, what time of year you air layered, and the plant's overall health.

It is important to monitor your air layers. Ants, birds, and bad weather can rip holes in the aluminum and plastic wrap causing the moss to dry out. If this happens earlier on, remoisten the moss and reapply new plastic wrap. If the stem and roots were left exposed too long, they will dry out and die, and may not be recoverable.

In two to six months, unwrap the aluminum foil. The roots will be visible through the plastic wrap. Cut off the rooted air layers at the bottom end for transplanting when the moss is fully packed with roots in late summer to early fall.

Prune off some of the top foliage to prevent the plant from being top-heavy and moving around in the pot. If too much foliage is left on the air layer, some of the older foliage will yellow and fall off. This may indicate that the plant is in shock, but it is not dying. It is adjusting to being removed from the mother plant.

In a shaded area out of the direct sun, carefully remove all the ties, aluminum and plastic wrap, leaving the mossy root ball intact. Also remove any stem left below the root ball.

Transplant into a pot that will accommodate the air layer's size. It is important that the plant does not move around in the pot or it will cause root damage. Again, use a well-drained soil, water every other day, and keep in a shaded area away from strong winds so the roots can take hold and grow into the soil.

In three to six months, when the roots grow to the bottom of the pot, the air layers are ready for repotting into a larger pot, or outplanting into the ground.

GRAFTING

Grafting involves the insertion of a short portion of stem, called a scion, into another stem with a strong root system, called the stock. The cambium layers (the cells producing new tissue) of the stock and scion must be placed tightly in contact with each other, and all parts being grafted must be related to one another in the same genus, or in some cases, the same family.

Grafting can be very useful for preserving those rare plants that fail to propagate by other, simpler methods. The time, skill, and complications involved in grafting mean that it is not recommended for plants easily propagated by other techniques. Grafting could help preserve species with bottlenecked populations on Hawai'i from being endangered. For example, for species with small individual or population numbers left, regeneration involves limited genetic material which can result in inbreeding. Inbreeding has caused some plants to become genetically weak and lose their ability to reproduce effectively. These weak plants have insufficient amounts of stored nutrients, their seeds are nonviable, and cuttings and air layers fail to root. Since future generations are in such peril, management measures that include grafting can be a good way to save them from extinction.

Kokia cookei grafted onto *K. kauaiensis* rootstock – NTBG — KRW

The grafting of native Hawaiian plants has been explored, but is not yet completely understood. A great deal of work has been done on the Malvaceae (hibiscus family). The rare *Kokia cookei* is a good example. It is a Moloka'i native, now extinct in the wild and surviving only in cultivation. Staff at Waimea Arboretum saved it by grafting it onto the rootstock of *Kokia drynarioides,* an endemic to North Kona, which is also endangered.

In 1998, I received some scion material of the *Kokia cookei* from Waimea Arboretum's mother plant. I used *Kokia drynarioides,* which was grown from seed, for the rootstock. I tried both top and side grafts; the top grafts worked the best. I also grafted the *Gardenia brighamii* from Moloka'i, of which there is one plant left in the wild, onto the same species of the O'ahu gene pool, which is not as threatened and produces many viable seeds.

Further work is being done at the NTBG on *Hibiscadelphus woodii,* a newer species endemic to Kaua'i, and *Kanaloa kahoolawensis,* a new genus and species from Kaho'olawe discovered by NTBG collectors, for which only one plant is left in the wild. Both of these species have difficulty reproducing themselves, most likely because of their isolation, inbreeding depression, and degraded, harsh environments; these factors stress the plants and result in weak growth. The *Kanaloa* is monotypic, meaning that the genus has only one species. Finding a compatible rootstock is quite challenging. Plants in the same family that closely resemble the *Kanaloa* were all considered. I used the *Pithecellobium dulce* (opiuma), an aggressive introduced coastal plant, as a rootstock, which was grown from seed. To date all of the grafts have failed to callus, and different plants are still being tested as compatible rootstock.

There have been many books written about grafting. I recommend thorough study of the subject and practice on non-native hibiscus hybrids before any attempt to graft threatened native plants.

Pteridophyte (Fern) Propagation

Hāpu'u tree fern – Kerin's yard — KJ

Fern spores are found from late spring to early fall on the undersides of fern fronds (fern leaves); many species have small round cases filled with spores called sporangia.

COLLECTING SPORES

Collect spores by picking a frond or piece of one with ripe sori (clusters of sporangia), which are usually either golden, dark brown, or black in color when ripe.

Place fronds in a clean, dry paper bag or between two sheets of paper. The spores will begin to drop within a day or two.

Sow spores right away for best results. Remember to label your plants and keep records.

STARTING SPORES

There are many different ways to start spores; this is what worked for me.

Use a clear, shallow container about the size of a shoebox, with no holes in it and an airtight lid.

Either use finely graded sphagnum moss, or hāpu'u (from tree ferns) and/or fine black cinder, any of these medias mixed together or by themselves.

Or you can use oasis cubes or a clean clay brick in the container, with ½ inch of distilled water in the bottom.

Sterilize everything to prevent fungi or algae growth from smothering the prothallia (young ferns). This can be accomplished by placing all of the materials in boiling water for ten minutes or longer.

Once the sphagnum moss (squeezed out), or hāpu'u and/or fine black cinder is cool enough to touch comfortably, spread it evenly in the container. Surface sow the spores lightly on top of the chosen material, then cover it. The lid should be airtight; this may require you to tape the seal if needed. Do not layer the spores densely on top of each other; this will waste spores and also hinder the development of the young ferns.

It is important not to let the moss, hāpuʻu, fine black cinder, or brick dry out at any time during the germination period. Moisture is needed to carry out the sexual fertilization procedure, which initiates the growth of the adult ferns. Your container should be airtight; be sure to mist with distilled water if drying out occurs. Temper-atures of 70°F (21°C) and above induce the best spore germination. Place the container in a protected, partially shaded area to prevent it from drying out. Be patient. In four to six weeks, depending on the species and the freshness of the spores, a green haze made up of many tiny clumps of prothalli (heart-shaped leaves) will form on the moss surface.

Fern propagation (oasis cube and plastic shoe box) — DR

Germinated fern spores — DR

TRANSPLANTING AND MEDIA

When these tiny ferns grow large enough, they are ready to be transferred into a sterile soil mix. The small true leaves, about the size of a pea, will be visible; this may take approximately six months. They are still vulnerable to diseases and drying out at this stage.

Fern transplant mixes

- 1 part potting mix to 2–3 parts perlite (1:3)
- 1 part potting mix to 3 parts fine, rinsed black cinder (1:3)
- Or 100 percent rinsed black cinder (good for plants under a mist system)

Very carefully and gently, without disturbing the roots, remove the small

Fern forest in Kerin's yard — KL

fern clumps, potting them into their own 1–2 inch pots, depending on the plant and root size. Water them in at first. The chlorine in some tap water can be harmful to the ferns at this early stage. Rainwater can be used as a substitute if it is pure. If possible, use distilled water for the first week, water every other day or when they become dry. Use tap water thereafter. For best results, keep the potted ferns under a mist system; if you do not have a mist system, a protected and shady area, off the ground and out of the wind, will also work. Be sure to monitor their growth and conditions often, and do not let the soil mix dry out at any time. Remember, the ferns just came out of a moist environment. Transplant them into 4–6 inch pots when the ferns become root-bound, usually within two to five months. Use the same mix recommended for rooted cuttings and seedlings.

Greenhouse

When maintained properly, a greenhouse provides a controlled environment that promotes maximum plant growth and development. There are five basic environmental factors that need to be maintained at the proper level, in order to grow healthy plants. They are:

- Moisture
- Soil temperature
- Oxygen
- Light
- Nutrients

Young plants and unrooted cuttings need this added protection from extreme weather conditions, diseases, insects, and hungry animals. It can shield them from such unwelcome visitors as slugs and rodents, which will eat the seeds and the tender seedlings.

Maile seedlings — KL

Greenhouse Management

Koa seedlings at Kaua'i DOFAW nursery — KL

MATERIALS

The glass greenhouses with elaborate heating and cooling systems, commonly used in temperate zones, are not necessary in tropical regions. Regions with mild year-round tropical climates, such as Hawai'i, need only a simple wood or metal-framed structure to provide good ventilation. This helps to control the temperature and humidity. It can also house wire-top benches, an irrigation system, potting mixes, and other materials. If a greenhouse is not available, a bench or table under a shade tree, closely monitored, can also produce fair results.

SHADE

A greenhouse structure should provide three levels of protection and shade.

- 50 percent shaded covered area

- 30 percent shaded open area
- Full-sun area

The propagation area ideally includes a solid, clear, plastic roof that provides about 50 percent shade. It can be used for germinating seeds, rooting cuttings, and caring for sensitive plants that need extra protection. It is also where a mist box or bench, which creates high humidity, would be best housed. This is also the best area for propagating plants from wetter environments, or green softwood, and herbaceous cuttings that need the extra moisture.

To protect the seeds and cuttings from pests, this area should be closed in with secure shade cloth walls. I have had problems with the melodious laughing thrush *(Garrulax canorus)* and rodents pulling out seedlings and cuttings while searching for insects in the media. It helped to have the entire propagation area enclosed.

Plants ideal for the 30 percent shaded open area include newly transplanted plants such as seedlings, rooted cuttings, air layers, and grafts that all need to be slowly hardened off as they adjust to more sun.

The open area with full sun and no roof or shade cloth is also useful to harden off plants and prepare them for transplanting out-of-doors.

Plants need these different growing conditions at different stages in their lives to help them become healthy and strong enough for outplanting into the ground, the ultimate goal. Native hardwood plants do not do well in pots for long periods of time. In general, I like to outplant them when they have outgrown a 4-inch pot (for ground covers and small shrubs), or a 1-gallon pot (for larger shrubs and trees), depending on the plant.

IRRIGATION
Irrigation is an important factor; overhead misting or hand watering should be done every other day. During the rainy season, water only the covered propagation area. Close monitoring of soil moisture is critical. Remember that overwatering can cause damping-off, which may kill seedlings. If possible, avoid using water from streams or lakes, which has too many contaminates. Rainwater is best, if it is pure.

SANITATION
Sanitation is an essential part of greenhouse management. Good sanitation can reduce or prevent plant diseases and the invasion of insects, pests, and weeds.

PEST AND DISEASE MANAGEMENT
Make sure that all new plant materials are disease and insect free before

they come into the propagation area. During germination and rooting periods, use pasteurized soil-less mixes to eliminate weed seeds and pathogen problems. Always use clean containers, flats, or pots; if they are soiled, wash them in a weak bleach solution of 1 part bleach to 10 parts water (1:10). Also disinfect the shears, knives, or any other tools used for propagation. Try to keep young plants elevated off the ground on benches and away from slugs, ants, and soil-borne diseases.

Slug on 'ōhi'a seedlings — KL

The floor of the greenhouse should always be free of plant debris and weeds. Keep pests from crawling up the bench legs, and keep hose nozzles off the ground where they might pick up disease patho-gens. This requires a commitment of time, but it is essential and worthwhile for the successful propagation of native Hawaiian plants.

CONTAINER PRODUCTION AND MAINTENANCE

If you prefer to keep your native plants in containers instead of outplanting them, here are some guidelines. Use the same medium that is recommended for transplanting. Transplant your container plants into larger pots every year, replacing the media or just changing the top layer of mix. If you

Lobelia niihauensis flowering – NTBG nursery — KL

see roots at the top of the media in the pot, this indicates that the plant is root-bound, and your native plant needs to be repotted.

Transplanting and Outplanting

Outplanted native Hawaiian garden – NTBG — CC

Transplanting and outplanting is best done in the rainy season. Your plants will be ready for outplanting or repotting when your seeds, cuttings, and other plant materials are well rooted, growing healthy, or have outgrown their pots. This is indicated when the roots fill the bottom of the pot, but are not root-bound. The roots of root-bound plants circle several times around the bottom of the pot or become visible at

Hibiscus waimeae root-bound damage — KL

the top of the media. Severely root-bound plants are short-lived; the circling roots strangle the trunk of the tree or larger shrub, eventually killing the plant. Outplant ground covers and small shrubs out of 4-inch pots, large shrubs and trees out of 1- or 2-gallon pots, before they become root-bound.

LOCATION

Give careful thought to the size and location of your plant site. Consider the type of plants you want and the conditions under which they thrive, and place your plants where the best combination of light, shade, moisture, and drainage prevail. Allow enough space between plants and structures for each plant to grow to maturity without overcrowding its neighbor or hitting a fence, roof, or other structure. I like to outplant the natives together in layered groups which can include a tree, a shrub, a subshrub, a fern, and a ground cover, rather then each plant by itself. It is easier to amend and maintain one large area than several smaller ones. Place the plant in the best setting for the plant — not the best setting for you. If the plants grow naturally in a wet or dry environment, try to meet those needs. Do not outplant cultivated native plants into the wild without the proper permission and proper information on the plant in question; otherwise, you may be harming the gene pool of a distinct species that occurs only in that particular area. Some native species hybridize very easily, cross pollinating within the first flowering season, which can result in cross-pollution of the wild gene pool and the production of hybridized seeds rather than pure, viable wild seeds, as nature intended. Especially in Hawai'i, there are many endemic species of flora found only on one island. Introducing a related native from another island into the wild can have very damaging results.

SOIL PREPARATION

Prepare your soil well ahead of planting time to provide the right texture and nutrients. Roots like a soil that is spongy enough to hold moisture, but porous enough to provide air spaces and good drainage.

NOTE: The more time and effort you put into preparing the plant site's soil, the less time and effort will be required for their upkeep in the future.

Healthy soil grows healthy plants. Insects such as nematodes and diseases are more likely to attack weak, sick plants.

Sandy soils

Sandy soils can drain too quickly, and can be amended by mixing in well-rotted organic materials such as peat moss, compost, and/or well-decomposed manure. Make sure these materials are well decomposed before planting. Be especially careful with raw chicken manure, which can burn plants and will take up extra nitrogen from the soil to help complete decomposition. Plant leaves will turn yellow and drop off.

Heavy soils

Heavy soils that form sticky lumps when wet, or hard clods when dry, have poor drainage, and need to have cinder, gravel, coarse perlite #3, or coarse rinsed sand (with salts rinsed out) added in.

SITE PREPARATION

To prepare a site to outplant, first dig a hole twice as wide as the pot the plant is in; wider for shallow-growing plants such as ferns, herbaceous plants, ground covers, and some subshrubs. Dig the hole a little deeper than the pot for tall trees and shrubs. Amend the soil dug out from the hole accordingly, and sprinkle a small amount of slow-release fertilizer into the bottom of the hole. Add some of the amended soil. Now it is time to carefully remove the plant from the pot by gently loosening the roots and some of the mix around the roots. If the plant is root-bound, carefully undo the circular growth pattern to prevent poor root growth, and place the plant in the hole with the roots directed downward (for trees). Fill in the remaining area with the amended soil and water. The water must drain freely for best results. It is important to outplant the plant at the same depth it was in the pot; plants (especially trees) can easily die by being planted too deep because the base of the stem or trunk will tend to rot. Be careful that the plant does not sink deeper into the hole after watering in, and over time. Gently pack soil around the plant to provide support; in windy locations, give extra support by tying the plant to a sturdy stake. Remove some of the lower leaves to reduce the effects of transplant shock. Make a moat or dam around the plant with the soil to keep the water from running off when watered. Water weekly when dry, until the plant becomes established, as indicated by new vegetative growth. After the plant is established, only water during prolonged periods of drought.

Polyacrylamide gel

When I worked for the Research Corporation of the University of Hawai'i (RCUH) in Köke'e, there was no source of water to irrigate the plants in the wild. In this situation, we used polymer, with great success. I highly recommend it as a soil amendment in similar situations.

Polyacrylamide powder (polymer) is a gel-like substance that swells up when water is added. If it is used properly, it can provide a water source for the plant for up to three to four years before breaking down. By this time the plant should be well established and have a healthy root system.

- Add 1 cup dry polymer to a 5 gallon bucket of water. For best results, let sit overnight or for several hours to swell.

- Use 1 cup of wet polymer for a 1-gallon pot size hole.
- Use ¼ cup to ½ cup for four to six-inch pot size. Mix the wet polymer and fertilizer into the soil dug from the hole before planting. Aways water in newly outplanted plants if water is available.

NOTE: In this case, more is not necessarily better. Too much polymer in the planting hole will swell excessively when it rains, and push the plant nearly out of the ground.

NUTRITION AND FERTILIZERS

Plant growth is highly responsive to the proper soil pH (5.0–7.0) and availability of nutrients.

- Nitrogen (N) stimulates new foliage, stem growth, and promotes the dark green color of leaves;
- Phosphorus (P) stimulates root growth, flowering, and fruiting;
- Potassium (K) stimulates overall plant strength;
- To adjust acid soil pH, add dolomite lime;
- To adjust alkaline soil pH, add sulphur.

Organic fertilizer, such as fish emulsion (5-1-1), applied every three to six months as a soil drench is excellent for ferns and sundew *(Drosera)* plants. Foliar feed your seedlings and other potted plants monthly with a water soluble fertilizer such as Miracle Gro® (15-30-15), fertilizing the plant through the foliage and the root system, helping them grow faster and greener. When leaves turn yellow from the lack of nitrogen and/or iron in the plant and surrounding soil, foliar feed with Miracid® (30-10-10) or iron-chelate fertilizers. This especially affects the species in the Rubiaceae and Santalaceae families. Slow release 8-8-8 NPK fertilizers work well for newly transplanted seedlings and smaller sensitive plants; for larger, older plants use a slow-release 10-10-10 NPK fertilizers. Depending on soil moisture, these fertilizers release gradually over a three to six month period, which reduces the possibility of injury from excessive use. Using organic fertilizers also reduces the injury to beneficial soil-borne fungi *(Mycorrhizae)* which live in and on the plant roots, helping them absorb much needed nutrients from the soil, and beneficial nematodes also living in the soil that feed on harmful insects that can damage and kill native plant roots ('ohai).

For a large outplanting, if the potential site soil conditions are uncertain, send a soil sample to your local Agricultural Extension Service. They will advise you on how to amend your soil for maximum growth and productivity.

To create a good soil sample, take a shovelful from five to eight places, evenly spaced within the prospective area. Mix the soil together and send a sample in the amount of whatever the local agricultural service requires to conduct their tests.

Outplanting in my yard — KL

Pest Control

PEST MANAGEMENT

Most pest control can be accomplished with a strong water spray from the hose while rubbing off the insects by hand. Native plants do not respond well to harsh insecticides; use botanical insecticides as much as possible. Since native Hawaiian plants evolved in isolation and were not exposed to aggressive herbivores, hoofed animals, and many insects, pests and diseases, they had little competition and lost or did not develop natural defenses or protection. The most damaging pests to cultivated native Hawaiian plants are the introduced insects: aphids, mealybugs, mites, scale, thrips, whiteflies, root-knot nematodes, and ants. Many of these attack the plants from the ground. These hungry insects do not have natural predators or freezing temperatures to keep them under control. Most of these insects thrive on plants with lush new growth caused by high nitrogen levels in the soil that are the result of over fertilization. This new growth is food for the sucking insects. They produce honeydew, which in turn is harvested by ants to feed their nestmates. Whatever pest management system you develop, keeping a consistent and regular application regime is an important part of keeping the pests under control.

Aphids cause foliage to become shriveled and wrinkled, and they also carry diseases (viruses) from plant to plant. They are tiny insects, usually dark green in color and yellow or black, and commonly feed on new growth. Management consists of applying systemic pesticides, neem oil, soap spray, or horticultural oil.

Hibiscus *erineum* leaf mite prefer the Chinese red hibiscus *(Hibiscus rosa-sinensis)*, but will also attack other hibiscus species, natives and introduced.

Hibiscus leaf mite on koki'o — KL

In Hawai'i it was first discovered on hibiscus in 1989 on Oahu, and it is now found on all the main islands. Adult hibiscus erineum leaf mites have soft worm-like bodies, invisible to the naked eye. Raised puckered bumps (galls) on the leaves are the plants reaction to the mite feeding. Young leaves and buds are most vulnerable to leaf mite infestation because new plant growth is necessary for mite establishment. (Insect Pests CTAHR April 2001 IP-7)

Mealybugs in large populations can cause a plant to shed its leaves and become stunted or even die. They appear as small puffs of cotton in the joints, the undersides of leaves, in the roots, or any protected crevice on the plant. Management includes applying systemic pesticides, neem oil, soap spray, or horticultural oil.

Mealy bugs — KL

Slugs eat the leaves and stems of the more herbaceous plants like *Brighamia*. To control them, use a granular slug bait—or remove them by hand and monitor the plants often, looking for indications such as slime trails.

Spider Mites suck chlorophyll from leaves, turning them pale green or yellowish, and cause them to fall off if they are left untreated. Webs occur on the leaves or in plant branch crotches; mites appear as tiny reddish specks moving about. *Brighamia* are particularly susceptible plants. To

Hibiscus snow scale — KL

manage spider mites, rotate the use of insecticides; the red spider mites become immune to the chemical within one generation. Rotate the use of mitecides, neem oil, soap sprays, or horticultural oil.

Scale infested plants are stunted and have yellow leaves. Their branches are ringed with scales, and they may die. Scale insects look like raised, brownish, black, or green spots along the stems and leaf ribs. Applying systemic pesticides, neem oil, soap spray, or horticultural oil can manage scale.

Thrips feed by scraping the undersurface of plant tissues and sucking up the juices that leak out. The leaves of thrip-infested plants appear silver with

Whitefly on **Hibiscus koki'o** leaves — MC

blackish spots, which is actually their fecal matter. Damage also occurs in the flowers, as in many of the *Hibiscus.* Thrips are very small blackish-brown insects with straight bodies. They can be managed by applying a systemic pesticide or by using horticultural oil. Yellow sticky paper traps help give an indication of what pests are in the area and can help reduce the insects that get trapped on them.

Whiteflies are small, white-winged insects that cluster on the under side of leaves and fly about when disturbed. Plants infested with whiteflies have leaves that turn yellow and fall off if left untreated. They are often in the *Hibiscus* family. To manage whiteflies, wash off the infested area of the plant by hand with a strong spray of water, or use systemic pesticides or horticultural oil.

Spittle Bug infestations resemble spit on the tips of the plants — so much so, that when I first saw them, I honestly thought that someone was spitting all over my plants. Small, green, round beetles live under the spit-like substance. To manage spit bugs, apply a systemic pesticide or wash them off by hand.

Chinese Rose Beetles eat holes in the leaves at night, and in severe cases, cause the plants to become weak because of the reduced amount of leaf surface, which the plant needs to conduct its photosynthesis. To easily manage rose beetles, set up solar night lights near the top of the plants, deterring the beetles, or apply a systemic pesticide, or use a bacterial

African snails — KL

insecticide (bacillus) to the plant to poison the beetles.

Black or **Coffee Twig Borers** are destructive little beetles that bore a small hole into the trunk or stem of plants. They lay their eggs in these holes, and when the larvae hatch out, they feed on the pith, causing the plant to die from the hole upwards, (young *Koa*). Cutting

Root-knot nematodes – ***Sesbania tomentosa*** root — DR

and burning the infested twig or stem will help control the borer, and some plants may grow back from below the bore hole. Plants are more susceptible to bore damage when stressed, unhealthy, or when tree seedlings are younger. Look for a tiny hole and a pile of fine powder in the soil below it. To manage this pest, keep the plants healthy and use a systemic pesticide.

Root-Knot Nematodes are parasitic, microscopic worms that live in the soil and roots of most plants. About a half-million species of nematodes exist in the world today. Some are beneficial, attacking and feeding on harmful insects, while others feed on plants and cause the roots to form galls, blocking the flow of water and nutrients to the plant above and leading to stunted growth, yellowing leaves, and wilt. Plants can take years to die. Fleshy-rooted plants such as *Hibiscus* and *Brighamia* seem to be the most affected. To manage nematodes, use a nematicide mixed into the soil at the time of outplanting. Follow the directions on the manufacturer's label closely, or soil drench with neem oil extracts every few months.

Ants are by far the most destructive pests to plants, in and out of the greenhouse. They farm sucking insects that weaken plants (such as aphids, scales, and mealybugs) for the honeydew these insects produce. The ants also protect these insects from their natural predators. You will have to control the ants first, and then the other insects. Use ant bait or insecticide at the base of the plant, being careful not to harm the plant with harsh insecticides. Be consistent with periodic application. If ants become a major problem, the mixture below is effective.

Bait for most Ants
1 ½   cups of tap water
1 cup white sugar (white works best)
1 tablespoon boric acid or borax
1 teaspoon creamy peanut butter
Mix in a blender until syrupy. Pour into containers.

Use small plastic containers with lids (such as containers for yogurt or sour cream) to dispense the ant bait. Put between two and four holes in the side of the container near the lid, large enough for the ants to enter. Fill half of the container with the bait mix and make sure the lid is on tight.

Place the containers near the ant holes and observe the worker ants. They will be attracted to it because of the sugar and or the peanut butter; they will sample the bait, and then take it home to the queen and the other ants in the nest. In a few weeks to a few months, depending on the size of the nest, the ants will succumb to the boric acid and dehydrate, die, or move away. I change the ant baits once a month, or when they are empty.

Rodents

Hawai'i has four introduced rodents: the roof rat, Norway rat, the Polynesian rat, and the common house mouse. All of them can be a major nuisance. They will forage on seeds and seedlings in the wild and in a nursery setting. The common signs of rodents are droppings and dig marks in and around the seed flats. To control them, use a trap set with fruit or strong smelling food (half-cooked bacon, peanut butter, or dried shrimp) and be consistent for the best results.

HORTICULTURAL OILS, NEEM, PYRETHRUM, OR INSECTICIDAL SOAPS

When used together or alone, horticultural oils, neem, pyrethrum or insecticidal soaps provide sufficient control for the insects discussed. Follow the directions on the manufacturer's label. Native plants are sensitive and can have adverse reactions such as phytotoxicity (when an insecticide is sprayed in the heat of the day, and it can burn the leaves and/or leave a persistent residue). To avoid this, spray in the morning or later in the day when it is cooler. For all pest control measures, consistency is key. As soon as you let up, they will be back and out of control, especially red spider mites. Be sure to rotate these insecticides for the best results.

Soap Spray
- Use Ivory Liquid® dish soap or Simple Green® liquid soap.
- Mix 1 part soap to 10 parts water (1:10)
- Apply with a liquid spray applicator

SYSTEMIC PESTICIDES

Systemic pesticides are granular insecticides that are taken up by plant roots. The chemical is then incorporated into the plant, and repels pests. Follow the directions carefully, and take care not to overdo it. I have used systemic pesticides on a wide range of native plants without casualties. Incorporate a small amount in the soil mix or sprinkle on the soil surface then water it in. The chemical must reach the root zone in order for the roots to absorb it. Systemic pesticides work particularly well on the Chinese rose beetle and the sucking insects mentioned.

MANUAL REMOVAL

For small outbreaks of insects, control can be achieved easily by rubbing the insects off by hand, accompanied by a strong spray of water from the hose. When watering, focus the spray to the underside of the leaves where the insects hide. This works well for small outbreaks of red spider mites or whitefly.

WEED MANAGEMENT

Weed management is important for the plant's health and growth. Weeds harbor pesky insects, and compete by taking up the much-needed moisture and nutrients intended for the native plants. At minimum, keep the base of plants weeded to help avoid herbicide and weed-eater damage, which will weaken or kill the plant.

Preemergent for weed control

Applying a preemergent for weed control works well for three to four months by preventing weed seeds from germinating, but it does not kill weeds already established. To apply, top-dress the granular chemical on the soil of potted plants or on the ground surface and water it in. Be consistent and pull any weeds before they flower. This will help you stay on top of weeds, especially during the rainy season. Stop using this product when the native plants mature and produce their own seeds; you will want to see if the seeds fall to the ground and regenerate themselves naturally. These seedlings can be potted or left to grow where they germinated, provided they have room to grow properly.

Herbicides

Native plants are sensitive to strong herbicides, so herbicides should be used with the utmost care. Avoid spraying weeds near the base of your plants. Some of these plants have shallow surface roots that help the plant take up more moisture from the soil, such as Koa trees; these roots may also take up the chemical and die. Do not spray on windy days; the drift may cause chemical burns to and/or kill nearby plants.

Weedy vines growing on 'akoko — KL

'A'ali'i

(Soapberry Family)

HAWAIIAN NAMES:
'A'ali'i; Kūmakani

GENUS:
Dodonaea

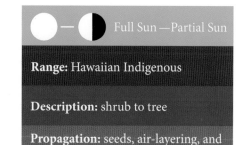

○ — ◐ Full Sun —Partial Sun

Range: Hawaiian Indigenous

Description: shrub to tree

Propagation: seeds, air-layering, and cuttings

Dodonaea viscosa seed capsules — HB

GENERAL DESCRIPTION

'A'ali'i occur in the wild from sea level to the high mountains. They grow as a many-branched, changeable shrub or tree, 1–30 feet tall. They will become more tree-like if given more shade and moisture. The narrow, short leaves are alternate and 1–4 inches long. The young leaf tips contain tannin, resins, were boiled and used for skin aliments by the early Hawaiians (Whistler 1992). Small inconspicuous greenish or red flowers form in clusters at the leaf axils or branch tips. They are unisexual, with either male or female flowers on the same plant or on different plants. The seed capsules are paper-thin, and are tan to dark red. They have two to four broad-winged angles that embody separate cells each containing a small round blackish seed. These attractive capsules were used in lei making and also to make a red dye. The dense, golden-brown hardwood was used for timber, weapons, and tools. These plants are good for a strong hedge, resistant to drought and wind. It is also good as an ornamental plant that can be trimmed and shaped to have a single trunk.

Entire Range: Pantropical-indigenous to Australia and all of the main islands of Hawai'i exc. Kaho'olawe

Wild Habitat: From coastal dunes, shrublands, dry, mesic and wet forests, to subalpine shrubland

Habit: Shrubs to small trees

Mature Height: 0.3–9 m height

Stem/Trunk: Stems are many branched, slender and straight, and the bark is reddish-brown to gray or blackish gray, and more or less sticky

Leaves: The leaves are variable: they are simple with entire margins, oval with pointed ends, papery to somewhat leathery, anywhere from 2–15 cm long by 0.5–6 cm wide. The leaves can be sticky to smooth, or sometimes with a slight covering of fine hairs, especially near the veins; they are green to mottled with red

Inflorescence/Flower: The flowers are unisexual, and the plant may have both male and female flowers on it or only male flowers; the flowers are lacking petals, in paniculate inflorescences, about 1–5 cm long, four sepals, eight stamens, female flowers have two to four styles

Fruit: The fruits are winged capsules, varying from a straw color to a rich, varnished red to purple; they can be compressed or inflated, two to four cells

Seed: Small, hard, dark, round seeds (Wagner et al. 1990)

PROPAGATION AND CULTIVATION SEEDS
- To propagate by seed, first collect the capsules when they are dry and tan or reddish and shedding from the plant.
- Keep them dry in a paper bag until they are ready to be cleaned.
- Separate the small black seeds from the capsules as directed for small dry seeds.
- The seeds can be stored in desiccation or at room temperature for up to eight years, however, it is best to start them fresh to achieve higher germination rates.
- Soak the seeds in hand-hot or tap water for twenty-four hours. The seeds will sink if they are viable; discard any floating seeds after the soaking time is up.
- Surface sow the small seeds onto a mix of 3 parts perlite to 1 part potting

mix or fine black cinder (3:1).

- Keep them moist, water them in, and then water every other day.
- Keep them in a covered area protected from heavy rains, which can disturb the seedlings.
-

GERMINATION

- Germination of all viable seeds can occur in two weeks to six months.
- Wait until four true leaves develop before transplanting them into 2-4-inch pots with a well-draining mix.
- The seeds take turns sprouting; it is best to re-move the seedlings as they germinate and keep the flat intact as more continue to germinate.
- Repot them into larger pots and new mix when they are twice as tall as their pots.
- Foliar feed them monthly, and move them into full sun to help harden them off and prepare them for outplanting.

CUTTINGS AND AIR LAYERING

Both of these methods work. However, I have found that by growing from seeds you can produce more plants that are stronger in the long run. I recommend propagation by seed unless seeds are not available.

OUTPLANTING

- Your 'a'ali'i will be ready for outplanting in about six months to a year or when they have outgrown a 6-inch to 1-gallon pot.
- Choose a site in the full to partial sun (they will grow taller in the shade).
- Amend the hole and soil to create a well-draining site by adding cinder or other coarse materials.

PESTS

Ants and their associated pests (scales, mealybugs, thrips, and aphids) can infest your 'a'ali'i; these sucking insects will feed on the plant juices. Use a systemic pesticide to control them and bait for the ants according to the protocols for ants.

ʻAeʻae

(Figwort Family)

HAWAIIAN NAME:
ʻAeʻae

COMMON NAME:
Water hyssop

GENUS:
Bacopa

○ — ◑ Full Sun — Partial Sun

Range: Indigenous

Description: herb and ground cover

Propagation: cuttings

Bacopa monnieri flowers — KJ

GENERAL DESCRIPTION

Bacopa is a creeping, succulent, perennial herb that is very adaptable to different habitats. They make a great ground cover, doing best when planted where they have their feet (roots) wet. This plant easily roots at the nodes, stabilizing the soil and deterring erosion; it grows into thick aquatic mats on or near marshes or brackish water streams; it even thrives on dried sandstone. The small, spatula-shaped, fleshy, opposite leaves are light green. Single pale-blue flowers develop from the leaf axils on top of long spikes; these form into small ovoid capsules containing tiny brown seeds. These plants are very easily propagated at any time of the year by collecting herbaceous cuttings. When using this plant as a ground cover, make sure you give it lots of room to roam. They have the tendency to take over an area if the soil is healthy and kept moist. I have some growing at 300 feet elevation and I need to keep trimming them away from growing up the hāpuʻu tree trunks.

Entire Range: Widespread in tropical and subtropical regions; Hawaiʻi: Midway Atoll, all main islands exc. Kahoʻolawe.

Wild Habitat: Occurs along coastal areas, mudflats, sand, bare sandstone, rocks, marshes, shores, or brackish streams

Habit: Perennial herb, semiaquatic

Mature Height: 1–6 dm long

Stem/Trunk: Prostrate stems, which root at the nodes and form mats

Leaves: Leaves opposite, with entire margins, fleshy spatulate leaves, and short leaf stalks

Inflorescence/Flower: Flowers are bell-shaped, solitary, with five lobes, corolla white to lilac or pale blue, and smooth, with two bracts beneath it. Flowers grow out of the leaf axils with the flower stalks up to 20 mm long

Fruit: Fruits are round capsules about 8 mm long and membranous

Seed: The seeds are numerous, pale brown, oblong, about 0.5 mm long, and with longitudinal ridges (Wagner et al. 1990)

PROPAGATION AND CULTIVATION CUTTINGS

- To propagate by cuttings, first collect herbaceous stem cuttings during the morning hours; keep them moist in a sealed plastic bag until they can be started; follow protocols for herbaceous stem cuttings.
- Remove the lower leaves, and cut the stems into 5-inch pieces, placing the bottom end under ½ inch of a mixture of 3 parts perlite to 1 part potting

mix (3:1), and water them in. No rooting powders are needed.

- Do not allow the mix to dry out; water them every other day, and they will develop roots in one to two months.
- Transplant the rooted cuttings one to three per 4-inch pot into a well-draining mix; water them in.
- Keep them in a shaded area for two weeks, then move them into full to partial sun to help harden them off.
- They will be ready for outplanting in five to six months.
- Foliar feed them monthly for strong, healthy growth.
- Large dug up clumps can be planted right into the ground; first, loosen the ground and cover the plants lightly with soil, then keep them moist until the roots become well established in the ground.

OUTPLANTING

- Choose a site in full to partial sun with moist, well-draining soil amended with cinder if the drainage is poor.
- Water them in after planting, and then water them when it is dry until they are well established, with their fast-growing roots holding the unstable soil in place.
- These flat, matted plants will grow to cover a large area, growing up and over other small plants. Simply trim them back if they get out of control.

PESTS

- Slugs may eat the leaves and the fruit; if you discover them, apply slug bait or pick them off by hand.
- Ants and their associated pests (scales, mealybugs, thrips, and aphids) can infest your Bacopa, these sucking insects will feed on the plant juices. Use a systemic pesticide to control them and bait for the ants according to the protocols for ants.
- This may only be a unique problem on the island of Kaua'i: wild chickens love to dig up the ground around the plants as they look for insects. They destroy the plants in the process because they expose the roots to the sun; the roots dry out and then die. If you have this problem, trap the chickens in live-traps and relocate them.

'Ākia
('Ākia Family)

HAWAIIAN NAMES:
'Ākia; Kauhi

GENUS:
Wikstroemia

Sun Requirements: Species specific

Range: Hawaiian Endemic

Description: ground cover, shrub or tree

Propagation: seeds and cuttings

'Akia seeds — KL

GENERAL DESCRIPTION

Native 'ākia occur scattered in the dry forests up to high alpine zones. They are low-growing subshrubs or small trees. Depending on the species and its habitat, the dark green or gray-green, shiny, opposite leaves are either small and ovate or large and narrow. Clusters of tiny, yellow, tubular, fragrant flowers develop at or near the branch ends from the leaf axils. The fruit ripens into round, pulpy, orange or red fruits, which are bird dispersed. There is one small blackish seed per fruit that is pointed at one end and has a somewhat hard seed coat, which protects the embryo. The roots and bark of W. *oahuensis* are believed to be poisonous (Stokes 1921, Degener 1945); Hawaiians used it to stupefy fish in small ponds. This is one of the few native Hawaiian plants with known active alkaloids. The Hawaiians used these plants occasionally for cordage; the fruit was used in leis, medicinally as a laxative and to treat asthma, and the softwood was used to make carrying sticks, called 'auamo (Abbott

Wikstroemia oahuensis fruit — JO

1992). This is a very easy plant to grow from mature seeds. Cuttings will root, but they take a little more effort to get them to root properly and readily. ʻĀkia is an attractive plant when used in the landscape with its many brightly colored fruits and gray-green foliage.

Entire Range: Hawaiian endemic

Wild Habitat: From dry forests to alpine zones

Habit: The habit is variable depending on the species; they can be prostrate, sprawling shrubs, subshrubs, or small trees

Mature Height: Variable from 1–10 m height

Stem/Trunk: Stems and branches have very strong fibers. Young branches may be covered with fine hairs or they may be smooth

Leaves: Leaves are opposite; the shape is variable from elliptic to oval, leathery, pale gray-green to dark green

Inflorescence/Flower: The flowers are perfect or unisexual, radially symmetrical, small, at stem apices or growing out of the leaf axils, flowers in inflorescences, calyx is four-lobed, flowers are tubular, petals are absent, and a nectary disk is present

Fruit: The fruit is an attractive, oval to round, pulpy drupe, which can be various shades of red to orange-red

Seed: There is one seed per fruit; they lack endosperm, have a hard seed coat, and are pointed at one end (Wagner et al. 1990)

PROPAGATION AND CULTIVATION SEEDS

- To propagate by seed, first collect the mature orange or red fruit when it is soft and shedding from the plant.
- Keep them moist in a plastic bag to help make the cleaning easier.
- Separate the pulp from the seeds as recommended for medium pulpy seeds.
- Start the seeds fresh to achieve higher germination rates.
- To pretreat the seeds, soak them in tap water for twenty-four hours.
- Sow the seeds onto a mix of 3 parts perlite to 1 part potting mix (3:1), water them in.
- Keep them in an area covered and protected from heavy rains.
- Water every other day or when dry.

GERMINATION

- All viable seeds will germinate in three weeks to five months.
- Sometimes a few seedlings will be completely white (albino) and short-lived because they do not have chlorophyll and cannot convert sunlight into food for the plant.
- Before transplanting the seedlings, wait until four true leaves develop.
- Transplant the seedlings into 2–4-inch pots, depending on the size of the root ball.
- Use a well-draining mix made of cinder, potting mix, and perlite.
- Repot them into larger pots when the seedlings are twice as tall as their pots.
- Keep them in the shade for a few weeks, then move them into more sun.
- The species from alpine zones, such as *W. phillyreifolia,* need to be cool and dry; the wet-forest species, such as *W. bicornuta* and *W. forbesii* need to be kept wetter and in a shady area; *W. uva-ursi* needs to stay drier and in full sun; this species is most commonly used in the landscape as a ground cover.

Wikstroemia uva-ursi seedling – NTBG nursery — KL

CUTTINGS

- To clonally propagate ʻākia by cuttings, collect the semi-hardwood tip cuttings about 4–5 inches long in the cool morning hours.
- Remove all lower foliage.
- Keep them moist in a sealed plastic bag until you start them.
- Remove ¼ -inch ring of the bark of the bottom end of the cuttings, then dip the end into rooting powder No. 8 or higher.
- Insert about 1 inch of the end into a moistened mix of 3 parts perlite to 1 part potting mix (3:1).
- Water the cuttings in lightly, so as not to wash off the applied rooting powder, but enough to settle the mix around cuttings.
- Keep them in a covered area and water every other day.
- They should root in about three to five months.
- Handle and care for your cuttings the same as described for the seedlings.

OUTPLANTING

- Your ʻākia will be ready for outplanting in six months to a year, when they have outgrown a 1–2-gallon pot.
- Choose a site similar to the wild habitat your ʻākia came from.
- They all need well-draining soil amended with cinder. Also, add a small amount of 8-8-8 NPK fertilizer to the soil.
- Water them in, and then water when it is dry until they are well established.
- ʻĀkia is an easy plant to take care of, and has few pest problems if it is planted properly.

PESTS

- Ants and their associated pests (scales, mealybugs, thrips, and aphids) can infest your ʻākia; these sucking insects will feed on the plant juices. Use a systemic pesticide to control them and bait for the ants according to the protocols for ants.
- Chickens can be pests because they eat the seeds from the pulpy fruits; they dig around the roots, exposing them, which dries them out. If you have chickens, be sure to collect the fruits before the chickens do.

'Akoko

(Spurge Family)

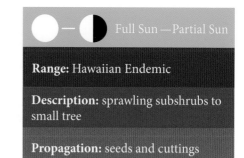
Full Sun —Partial Sun

HAWAIIAN NAMES:
'Akoko; 'Ekoko; Koko; Kōkomālei

GENUS:
Euphoribia (Syn: *Chamaesyce*)

Range: Hawaiian Endemic
Description: sprawling subshrubs to small tree
Propagation: seeds and cuttings

Chamaesyce celastroides var. kaenana seed capsules – O'ahu — SP

GENERAL DESCRIPTIONS

'Akoko is a very adaptable species and can grow as sprawling prostrate mats, subshrubs, to small trees. In dry coastal locations the plants are low-growing with smaller gray leaves that reflect the strong sunlight; salt spray and their stems store water for drier days. The 'akoko from higher elevations take on a tree-like growth with larger 6-inch long dark green, leathery leaves adapted to more moisture and shade. The seeds are even different: coastal 'akoko have tiny mucilaginous seeds, whereas inland species have larger drier seeds. These plants can become weedy in a nursery setting and when outplanted, which is a good thing for the plants; the seedlings can be transplanted or easily potted for elsewhere.

Entire Range: Hawaiian endemic

Wild Habitat: Open, dry, mesic, diverse mesic, to wet forests and rarely bogs; coastal vegetation, strand vegetation at sea level; dry shrubland, open sub-alpine, arid volcanic cliffs, and cloud-swept summit ridges

Habit: Herbs, subshrubs, large shrubs, or small trees

Mature Height: 0.5–9 m in height

Stem/Trunk: Herbaceous to woody, often with milky sap

Leaves: Leaves are simple, opposite, decussate (opposite leaves set at right angles to previous pair) or distichous (two-ranked, two opposite rows in the same plane), glabrous (smooth) or pubescent (with hairs), margins entire or serrate (toothed), leaf base usually asymmetrical, sessile (without a stalk) or subsessile, and with well-developed stipules.

Inflorescence/Flower: Monoecious, pistillate flowers (female) solitary, sepals and petals absent, ovary with three carpels and one ovule per cell; staminate flowers (males) in fives or cymules, with one to several flowers, sepals and petals absent

Fruit: Capsule with a persistent axis (rachis)

Seed: Seeds small (0.15 cm diameter) to larger (2.5 cm diameter), without an appendage near the seed hilum (ecarunculate), rounded to angled, seed coat mucilaginous, smooth to rugose (appears sculpted, like a brain), or marked with transverse or longitudinal grooves, with a copious endosperm (Wagner et al. 1990)

PROPAGATION AND CULTIVATION SEEDS (EASY)

- To propagate by seed, first collect the capsules when they are dry and turn brown or red; keep them dry in a paper bag until you are ready to clean and plant them.
- The seeds should be cleaned as directed for small dry seeds.
- Seeds can be stored up to four years in desiccation or kept dry in the refrigerator.
- Surface sow the small tan seeds on a dry mix of 3 parts perlite to 1 part potting mix (3:1); water the seeds in.
- For larger seeds cover with ½ inch of the same mix and water them in.
- Keep them in a covered, protected area until they germinate, then move the seedlings into an area with more sunlight.
- Water every other day or every two days. Keep the high elevation species, such as *E. remyi* and *E. rockii,* wetter.

GERMINATION

- Germination may take three days to two months for all viable seeds to sprout. They will be ready to transplant when at least four true leaves appear (in about a month).
- Use a well-draining mix for the drier and lower elevations species by adding more cinder or perlite. Use a wetter mix for the higher elevation species by adding more potting mix to the well-draining mix.
- Keep the seedlings in a shaded and protected area, and then move the lower elevation species into full sun and the high elevation species into partial sun.

Chamaesyce celastroides four month-old seedling – NTBG nursery — KL

CUTTINGS

- Take the semi-hardwood to softwood cuttings and remove all of the lower foliage, keeping the cuttings moist in a sealed plastic bag.
- Start the cuttings as fresh as possible, in a shallow flat of leveled mix made up of 3 parts perlite to 1 part vermiculite (3:1), or in 3 parts black cinder to 1 part potting mix (3:1).
- For semi-hardwood cuttings use rooting powder No. 3; for softwood cuttings use rooting powder No. 1 or none, depending on how green the stems are.
- Keep in a shaded, covered area and water every other day.
- Transplant the rooted cuttings in two to six months, which all depends on the stored food in the stems of the plant material collected.
- Pot the cuttings into well-draining soil and handle them the same as described for the seedlings.

OUTPLANTING

- 'Akoko may be ready for outplanting in six months to a year or when it outgrows a 4-inch pot for the low-growing 'akoko, and a 1-gallon pot for the taller tree 'akoko species.
- Choose a site in full to partial sun depending on which species; the higher elevation species need more moisture and shade, and the coastal species need full sun and drier locations.

- Fertilize the plants about every six months for healthy growth.
- The ʻakoko seeds will freely sprout and grow in the planting area or even in the pots; unwanted seedlings are easily potted up or can be relocated.

PESTS
- If ants infest your plants, control them from the base of the plant as recommended.
- Root mealybugs can be a problem. Control them with systemic pesticides (soil drench), or apply horticultural oils.

ʻAkoko — F&KS

Alahe'e

(Coffee Family)

HAWAIIAN NAMES:
Alahe'e; 'Ōhe'e; Walahe'e

GENUS:
Psydrax (Syn: *Canthium*)

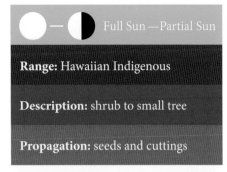

○ — ◑ Full Sun—Partial Sun

Range: Hawaiian Indigenous

Description: shrub to small tree

Propagation: seeds and cuttings

Psydrax (Canthium) odoratum flowers – NTBG — DR

GENERAL DESCRIPTION

Alahe'e is a small, attractive tree that can reach about 20 feet in height. In the wild, it grows in drier shrublands and forests. The thick glossy, opposite leaves are 2–3 inches long. They glisten in the sunlight and are pointed at both ends. Small, white, fragrant, funnel-shaped flowers cluster at the branch ends as do the small, blackish-green fruit clusters. These small, black, curved seeds are often attacked by a seed borer (on O'ahu), which bores a small hole into the embryo to lay its eggs. When they hatch, the larvae feeding on the seed kill it. If you experience this problem, spray the seeds as soon as they develop with an insecticide, then bag them until they ripen. The Hawaiians used the very hard dense wood for 'ō'ō, and sharp-edged adze blades that were used to cut other softer woods, and a black dye was made from the leaves (Wagner et al. 1990). These trees are very easy to germinate and maintain in the landscape. They can be used as a hedge or specimen tree. They make a good native substitute for mock orange (*Murraya* sp.) hedges.

Entire Range: Indigenous to Micronesia, the South Pacific, New Hebrides, New Caledonia, east to the Tuamotus, and in Hawai'i, all of the main islands exc. Ni'ihau

Wild Habitat: Dry shrublands, mesic to wet forests

Habit: Shrub or small tree

Mature Height: 3–6 m height

Stem/Trunk: The wood is durable, hard and was utilized by Hawaiians for tools

Leaves: Leaves are opposite, leathery, glossy on the upper surface, duller on the lower surface, leaves oval to lance-shaped, narrowed at each end. Stipules occur between leaf stalks.

Inflorescence/Flower: Small white flowers are fragrant, perfect or functionally female, occurring in crowned clustered cymes, flower corolla four- to six-lobed, stamens extending beyond petals. Nectary disc fringed with fine hairs

Fruit: The fruit is black, pulpy-juicy, roundish, with a groove on each side, and about 9 mm long

Seed: Seeds are black and incurved (Wagner et al. 1990)

PROPAGATION AND CULTIVATION
SEEDS

- To propagate by seed, first collect the ripe fruits when they are blackish and shedding from tree in the fall; keep them moist and soft in plastic bag until they are cleaned.
- Remove the pulp as recommended for medium pulpy seeds.
- Do not store the seeds; pretreat them with a soak in hand-hot or tap water for twenty-four hours. After the twenty-four-hour period, the viable seeds should sink; throw away any seeds that float.
- Sow them onto a mix of 3 parts perlite to 1 part potting mix (3:1),

Psydrax (Canthium) odoratum fruits — HB

then cover them with an additional ¼ inch of mix and water them in.
- Keep them in a covered, shaded area that is protected from heavy rains.
- Once they sprout, foliar feed them monthly.

GERMINATION
You can expect all viable seeds to germinate in about one to four months; wait until at least four true leaves develop before transplanting.

When they are ready to transplant, put them into tall 2-4-inch pots giving the roots ample room to grow down. Do not allow these trees to become root-bound in their pots.

Use a well-draining mix with small amounts of 8-8-8 NPK fertilizer.

Keep them in a shaded area, and repot the seedlings into larger pots about every four months.

Move them into full sun to help harden them off and prepare them for out-planting.

Foliar feed them monthly with Miracid® if the leaves yellow.

OUTPLANTING
- Your alaheʻe will be ready to outplant in about ten months to a year, when they have outgrown a 1–2-gallon pot.
- Choose a site protected from strong winds that is in full to partial sun.
- Amend the planting hole to create good drainage and add small amounts of 8-8-8 NPK fertilizer.
- Water your plants in, and then water them monthly until they are established.
- These trees need little to no care if they are planted in the right environment. Sometimes the foliage may yellow; if it does, foliar feed them with Miracid®, or soil drench them with chelated iron to add extra iron to the surrounding soil.

PESTS
- Ants and their associated pests (scales, mealybugs, thrips, and aphids) can infest your *Psydrax;* these sucking insects will feed on the plant juices. Use a systemic pesticide to control them and bait for the ants according to the protocols for ants.
- The seeds are sometimes attacked by native seed weevils that bore into the embryo and feeds, rendering the seeds nonviable. Use a systemic pesticide amended into the soil around the tree or bag the fruit when young until they ripen to prevent this.

Aloalo

(Mallow Family)

HAWAIIAN NAMES:
Aloalo; Hau Hele; Koki'o Kea; Koki'o
Ke 'Oke'o; Ma'o Hau Hele; 'Akiohala;
Koki'o; Koki'o 'Ula; Pāmakani

GENUS:
Hibiscus

Full Sun—Partial Sun

Range: Hawaiian Endemic

Description: shrub to tree

Propagation: seeds, air-layering, grafting, and cuttings

H. a. subsp. **punaluuensis** — KL

Hibiscus brackenridgei —DR

H. newhousei flower & seeds — KL

Hibiscus furcellatus – Maui — F&KS

GENERAL DESCRIPTION

The endemic *Hibiscus* species of the Hawaiian Islands are believed to be the result of four independent colonization events. They occur in dry to wet forests on all the main islands as shrubs to tall trees. Flowers can be white, yellow, orange, or red, depending on the species. *Hibiscus* is the easiest genus to grow and maintain in the landscape. It is readily grown from seeds, cuttings, air layering, and/or grafting. The uniquely beautiful flowers of the *Hibiscus* make this one of my favorite plants to propagate and grow.

Yellow H. k. saintjohnianus — KL

H. kahilii — KL

H. kokio – kipu kai — KL

4 petaled *H. saintjohnianus* — KL

(left) *H. ssp. immaculatus,* (top right) *H. waimeae,* (bottom) *H. ssp. hannerae* — KL

Range: Hawaiian endemic

Wild Habitat: Dry, mesic to wet forests

Habit: Subshrubs, shrubs to trees

Mature Height: 1–10 m in height

Stem/Trunk: Woody and branching with smooth to pubescent (hairy) stems

Leaves: Leaves are simple, with leaf stalks, stipules, leaves usually not lobed but some species with palmately lobed leaves; margins entire to toothed; leaf surfaces smooth and glossy to soft and covered with a surface of fine hairs

Inflorescence/Flower: Flowers solitary, growing from the leaf axils or at the ends of the branches, flower parts in multiples of five, staminal column, five-celled ovary, petals with a wide array of colors including white, yellow, pink, red, and orange. Some species of Hawaiian *Hibiscus* flowers produce a fragrance

Fruit: A capsule with locular chambers, each splitting open at maturity

Seed: Seeds angular-kidney-shaped and either smooth or covered with hairs (pubescent) (Wagner et al. 1990)

PROPAGATION AND CULTIVATION SEEDS

- To propagate from seeds, first collect the brown seed capsules when they are mature and starting to split open.
- Keep them dry in a paper bag until cleaning. Prepare them as soon as possible to prevent any insect damage, such as from seed weevils.
- Seeds can be stored at room temperature, refrigerated, or in a desiccation chamber, but viability is higher if you start with fresh seeds.
- Soak the small fuzzy seeds in tap water for twelve to twenty-four hours; the seeds should sink after the soaking time.
- Sow them onto a mix of 3 parts perlite to 1 part potting mix (3:1), cover the seeds with ½ inch of additional mix, then water them in.
- Keep them moist in a covered area; watch for slugs, which will eat the seedlings.

GERMINATION

- It can take from five days to three months for all viable soaked seeds to germinate.
- Wait until at least four true leaves develop before transplanting, then transplant into 2–4-inch pots, depending on the size of the root balls.

- Keep the seedlings in a shaded area, slowly moving them into a sunnier area to harden them off.
- Repot into larger pots when they become twice as tall as pots they are growing in; it is important that the plants do not become root-bound at any time. Root-bound plants can result in poor root systems that will eventually kill the plants.

Hibiscus clayi seeds and capsules – NTBG — MC

- Foliar feed them monthly and add small amounts of 8-8-8 NPK fertilizer every three to six months.

CUTTINGS
- Follow the directions for all the types of cuttings; all types work with *Hibiscus*. My preference is to use hardwood cuttings with rooting powder Nos. 3–8.
- Your cuttings will root in about three to five months depending on the health of the parent plant.
- Handle and care for the cuttings the same as described for the seedlings.

AIR LAYERING
- Follow the directions for air layering and handling; use rooting powder Nos. 8–30, as all work well.
- Roots should develop in about three to five months.

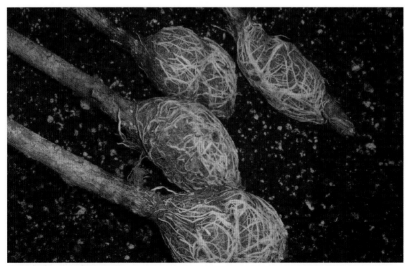
Rooted Hibiscus air layers — KL

GRAFTING

- Grafting is a specialty technique in itself. If you are unfamiliar with grafting, refer to the many books and resources available on grafting techniques first. Here I will describe how to apply these techniques to the Hawaiian *Hibiscus* species.
- First, prepare your rootstock by growing *Hibiscus rosa-sinensis* (common red hibiscus) for the best rootstock. This can be grown from seed or hardwood cuttings. Keep the rootstocks from becoming root-bound by repotting as they grow; this will reduce or eliminate damaging the root system. Do not graft onto a newly repotted rootstock because it is still weak.
- Native *Hibiscus* can *also be used for rootstock. For example, H. waimeae subsp.* hannerae can be grafted onto *H. waimeae* subsp. *waimeae* as the rootstock. These can then both be allowed to grow out and display both blossoms. Another extraordinary result can be obtained from grafting all of the different colors of *Hibiscus kokio* subsp. *saintjohnianus* flowers onto one rootstock.
- Follow the directions for grafting as described in the many books on the subject.
- It can take three to five months for grafts to callus over.
- Repot them when the plants are twice as tall as the pots they are growing in.
- Foliar feed them monthly and apply small amounts of 8-8-8 NPK fertilizer.

OUTPLANTING

- It will be six months to a year before your *Hibiscus* is strong enough for outplanting.
- Choose a site in partial to full sun and out of strong winds.
- If the roots are circling around in the pot, undo them and carefully try to get them to grow straight down into the planting hole. If the circling roots are not corrected, they will grow around the shrub, eventually strangling the plant and killing it within a few years.
- Plant *Hibiscus* with other plants, ground covers, and subshrubs.
- Amend the site to create a well-draining soil; fertilize the area as recommended.
- Water in the plants, then water them weekly depending on the rainfall, until they are well established and are growing healthily.
- Foliar feed them every two months and add small amounts of 8-8-8 or 14-14-14 NPK fertilizer amended into the surrounding soil.

H. brackenridgei – scale — KL

PESTS

- Ants and their associated pests (scales, mealybugs, and aphids) can infest your *Hibiscus* plants; use a systemic pesticide and control them according to the protocols for ants.
- Chinese rose beetles eat the leaves, reducing photosynthesis and stressing the plant; apply a systemic pesticide as recommended.
- Whiteflies and snow scale can infest your *Hibiscus*; if they do, wash them off with a strong water spray or spray with horticultural oil.
- Red spider mites can take up residence on the underside of the leaves. If they do, spray your plants with horticultural oil.
- *Hibiscus* erineum mite control as recommended, in Pest Management.

Ālula
(Bellflower Family)

HAWAIIAN NAMES:
Ālula; ʻŌlulu; Puaʻala

GENUS:
Brighamia

Partial Sun

Range: Hawaiian Endemic

Description: succulent

Propagation: seeds

Ālula, Limahuli Gardens — KL

GENERAL DESCRIPTION

The two endemic *Brighamia* are very un-usual, different from all of the other gen-era in Hawaiʻi. They have thick, succulent stems, stout at the base, which support this sometimes tall plant (3–15 feet). In most cases, the leaves form a single rosette at the top, but sometimes if the tip is damaged the plant will branch out, forming up to three or more rosettes. The leaf rosette consists of either large or small leaves depending on the amount of sun and moisture available to the plant. Fragrant long white to yellow flowers

Brighamia rockii flowers – Molokaʻi — SP

form in late summer within and just above the leaves. Seeds develop in green capsules in some cases all year long, splitting when they mature. Lines of latex form along the splits on the capsules, which can glue the seeds to insects or the feathers of birds. This is a dispersal mechanism and how they probably arrived.

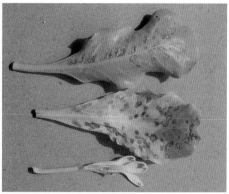

Brighamia insignis leaves affected with leaf spotting fungus — MC

The thick succulent stem holds water for times of drought; overwatering can easily rot and kill ālula. If the stem starts to soften at the top or near the base; this indicates problems. Check the media at the base of the plant. If it is wet, stop watering because too much water has caused the stem to start to rot. If the soil is dry, continue to water, as the stem is soft because it has dried out. The plant may grow out of this stage of decline; too much water can also cause fungal infection on the foliage indicated by brownish-yellow spots on the leaves. The infected leaves should be removed and destroyed. Goats are a major threat to ālula in the wild because they feast on the succulent stem, which is the reason why only plants isolated on steep cliffs survive today, and most of their seeds fall into the ocean below.

Fortunately, these are very easy to grow in cultivation. In fact, they have become quite popular with succulent plant enthusiasts nationally and internationally. Seeds distributed from Hawai'i in the 1970s were recently traced and their progeny were found in many botanic gardens and private gardens around the world. I have seen *Brighamia* growing in a botanic garden in Switzerland. Treat the ālula like a succulent; giving it partial sun, a well-aerated soil mix, a little water, and lots of tender loving care.

Entire Range: Hawaiian endemic

Wild Habitat: Sea cliffs, windward cliffs 0–470 m elevation

Habit: Succulent, solitary or branched stem with rosette of leaves at apex

Mature Height: 1–5 m

Stem/Trunk: Solitary to branched succulent 1–5 m tall. Stout stems, fleshy, thickened toward the base, glabrous (smooth), the stem is not truly woody; it is soft

Leaves: Simple, arranged in a dense apical rosette; fleshy, obovate (inversely

Brighamia insignis capsules and seeds — KL

ovate), margins entire, slightly toothed, sessile (attached without a stalk) to subsessile

Inflorescence/Flower: Fragrant, three to eight in suberect to horizontal racemes; corolla white or yellow, the tube slender, straight, entire at anthesis, ovary inferior, two-celled; each cell dehiscent by two lateral slits

Fruit: Capsules 13–20 mm long and 4–10 mm wide

Seed: The seeds are very tiny, numerous, pale, and ovoid (Wagner et al. 1990)

PROPAGATION AND CULTIVATION SEEDS (EASY)

- To propagate by seeds, first collect mature capsules when the latex is present along the splits on the swollen capsules.
- Keep the capsules dry in a paper bag until they are cleaned. Remove the small seeds by ripping capsules apart above a bowl; this will help avoid

Brighamia insignis 100 day old seedling – NTBG nursery — PT

losing any seeds.

- Sow the seeds fresh for best results. Do not desiccate them (they will lose their viability), but they can be stored dry in the refrigerator up to a year.
- No pretreatments are necessary; surface sow the small seeds onto a mix of 3 parts perlite to 1 part potting mix (3:1); or use 3 parts fine black cinder to 1 part potting mix (3:1).
- Water the seeds in, and keep them in a covered, protected area; watch for slugs, which like to eat the seedlings.

Brighamia insignis F1 seeding – NTBG nursery — KL

GERMINATION

- Germination begins in ten days. They will start to develop into tiny sprouts, and in another three months all of the viable seeds will have germinated.
- Foliar feed the seedlings monthly with a light solution. Transplant them into 1–2-inch pots when they are only ½ inch tall.
- It is important that the transplant mix is free-draining; use 3 parts fine black cinder to 1 part potting mix (3:1) with a small amount of 8-8-8 NPK fertilizer mixed in; or 3 parts perlite to 1 part potting mix (3:1).
- Keep potted seedlings in a shaded area for two to three months. Maintain on the dry side, watering twice a week or when dry. It is important not to disturb the roots; pot them with care
- Repot them into 4-inch pots in two to three months, then repot them every six months using new media and larger pots. Cement or clay pots are recommended to help keep the soil on the dry side, a mix of 3 parts black

Ālula – KL

cinder to 1 part potting mix (3:1) with small amounts of 8-8-8 NPK fertilizer mixed in is recommended.

OUTPLANTING

- In general, *B. rockii* is harder to keep alive in cultivation. It seems to be weaker and more susceptible to various pests, diseases, and other potential problems.
- *B. rockii* is ready for outplanting in two years; *B. insignis* may be ready in one year.

Slug on Ālula — KL

- *B. insignis* and *B. rockii* will tolerate partial sun, doing best on the northeast side of a building or yard.
- Some of the best sites for planting this remarkable but sensitive plant include black cinder rock gardens or in mounds of cinder reinforced with large rocks.
- Be careful not to bruise the soft stem; a bad bruise can cause rotting to set in, and, eventually, death. Use a fungicide to treat any wounds in the stem if they occur from slugs or other pests.
- *Brighamia* does well as a container plant if it is transplanted into larger pots when needed.

PESTS

- Ālula has two major pests: slugs, which can be managed using slug bait; red spider mites, which can be managed using horticultural oils.
- Slugs can even kill large plants by eating holes into their succulent stems, which succumb to fungal rot; if this happens, treat the holes in the stem with a fungicide.
- Red spider mites live on the underside of leaves, turning the leaves yellow. If left untreated, the leaves will fall off and weaken the plant. Wash off the mites by hand for small outbreaks.

Hala

(Screw Pine Family)

HAWAIIAN NAMES:
Hala; Pū Hala

GENUS:
Pandanus

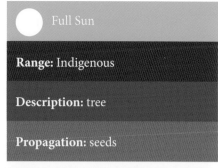

Full Sun

Range: Indigenous

Description: tree

Propagation: seeds

Pandanus tectorius with fruit — AW

GENERAL DESCRIPTION

The very useful hala tree occurs from coastal habitats to inland mesic valleys. It grows 20–35 feet tall, with many thick aerial roots (ulehala) protruding down from the trunk to the ground, making it seem like the hala tree could walk away at any time. The long leaves (lau hala) are crowded at branch ends in a spiral, with sharp prickles along the edges. Male flowers extend out in a spike, and are surrounded by very fragrant, long, pointed, whitish, edible bracts. The yellow to red edible drupes (pua hala) form in clusters of about fifty at the end of the branches. They look a lot like pineapples growing in the tree. One to three embryos are present in each seed, and sometimes they all sprout at once. Hawaiians made mats, baskets, sandals, pillows, and thatching from the leaves, and sometimes ate the seeds (Wagner et al. 1990). Hala is a fast and easy tree to grow for a coastal planting from the plentiful seeds.

Entire Range: Indigenous to Pacific islands of Polynesia, Melanesia, Micronesia, also New Caledonia to northern Australia, New Guinea, west to the Philippine Islands, Moluccas, and Java; in Hawai'i, on all main Hawaiian islands except Kaho'olawe

Wild Habitat: Mesic coastal regions, from sea level, growing in groves, low elevation mesic slopes, further inland and rarely higher than 610 m elevation.

Habit: Small tree

Mature Height: Reaching 12 m height

Stem/Trunk: Ascending trunk with conspicuous leaf scars, dichotomously branching (branching in twos), or trichotomously (in threes); base of trunk is supported by prop roots, which are sometimes armed

Leaves: Leaves are green (usually), simple, 3-ranked, spiraled, crowded at the branch ends; they can have sharply toothed to smooth margins; they are leathery, smooth, linear, sometimes twisted and from ca. 80-180 cm long, and ca. 408 cm wide. The leaf midrib is keeled on the lower side.

Inflorescence/Flower: Unisexuale (female and male flowers on same tree), terminal inflorescences, with white to cream colored bracts, flowers unisexual with perianth absent, flower parts in multiples of three, four-celled anthers, stamens connate into bundles (male), carpels connate into phalanges, with one ovule per carpel (female), inflorescence a solitary head, closely enveloped by bracts.

Fruit: Polydrupes with five to eleven cells, pericarp yellowish to orange-red when ripe, fleshy-fibrous, endocarp reddish brown and bony. Each fruit is called a "key" and will often begin to sprout right on the ground. A fruiting head has been said to resemble a pineapple growing in a tree.

Seed: Seeds are large, 8–15 mm long, and fusiform-ellipsoid, dispersed mostly by salt water flotation (Wagner et al. 1990)

PROPAGATION AND CULTIVATION SEEDS

- To propagate from seeds, first collect the drupes (fruits) when they are yellowish to red in color and are shedding from the tree.
- Keep them moist in a plastic bag for easy pulp removal.
- Wash the thin layer of pulp off by hand with a scrubber, or clean them as recommended for large pulpy seeds.
- Start the seeds fresh for higher germination rates.
- Soak the seeds in tap water for twenty-four hours. The seeds will float (that is how they traveled to the islands).
- Sow them in a shallow flat on a mix made up of 3 parts perlite to 1 part potting mix (3:1), cover the seeds with about one additional inch of mix, then water the seeds in.
- Keep the flats in a shaded area, and water every other day.

GERMINATION

- Germination will take from one to four months for all viable seeds to sprout; wait until at least four true leaves develop before transplanting them into 4-inch pots using a well-draining mix.
- Keep the seedlings in the shade for a week or so, then move them into full sun.
- Repot them into larger pots in four to six months; make sure the roots do not become root-bound.

OUTPLANTING

- Your hala will be ready for outplanting in about nine to twelve months, or when they have outgrown a 1-gallon pot.
- Choose a site in the lower elevations with full sun and a well-draining soil; amend the ground as directed.
- Water them in, then water weekly when the ground is dry until you observe new growth, then only water in times of prolonged drought.
- Fertilize every six months for healthy growth.
- These are easy, hardy plants to care for; I even have some planted in lava rocks bonsai-style.

PESTS

Ants and their associated pests (scales, mealybugs, and aphids) can infest your hala plants; use a systemic pesticide and control them according to the protocols for ants.

Hōʻawa

(Pittosporum Family)

HAWAIIAN NAMES:
Hōʻawa; Hāʻawa

GENUS:
Pittosporum

Hōʻawa seeds — KL

GENERAL DESCRIPTION

Hōʻawa occur in dry, mesic, wet, to subalpine forests. They are quite attractive evergreen shrubs and trees that can be used as landscape ornamentals. The narrow leaves cluster at the branch ends and are sometimes covered with fine brownish hairs (tomentose). Small whitish flowers (perfect or unisexual) are borne along the stems, just below the leaves or in the leaf axils. The large oval woody seed capsules are 2–3 inches long and brightly colored, yellow to orangish-red on the inner surfaces. They contain ten to twenty shiny, sticky orange or blackish seeds that attract birds. The seeds were dispersed to the Hawaiian Islands by birds, either in their stomachs or stuck to their feathers. The capsules have evolved to become much larger than when they first arrived to the islands. This loss of dispersibility is characteristic of island species (Carlquist 1980; Grant 1998). The endemic crow, ʻalalā, that is nearly extinct,

Pittosporum hosmeri flowers — KL

used P. *hosmeri* as a source of food (Neal 1965). It was easy for it to open the woody seed capsules with its strong beak. *Hōʻawa* is an easy plant to propagate and maintain in the landscape although it is slow-growing.

Entire Range: Hawaiian endemic

Wild Habitat: From dry, mesic, wet and subalpine forests to diverse mesic forests, open bogs, valleys, and coastal woodlands

Habit: Shrub to tree

Mature Height: 1–14 m

Stem/Trunk: Pubescent (covered with fine hairs and/or glands), or smooth

Leaves: Leaves are simple, alternate, usually clustered at branch ends, leathery, entire leaf margins or toothed; or margins rolled over at the edges

Inflorescence/Flower: Flowers are perfect or unisexual (either entire plant male or female or a species has both male and female flowers on the same plant); radially or irregularly symmetrical; flowers occur from the axils, or terminal inflorescences; petals in fives, which are white, cream, yellowish-purple, or red. Flowers form a corolla tube.

Fruit: Fruits are capsules which are smooth to wrinkled with a persistent style, the exocarp (outer layer of fruit) is leathery to woody, and the inner layer is fleshy.

Seed: Seeds numerous, black to reddish-black, and sticky (Wagner et al. 1990)

Rats eat hōʻawa seeds — KL

PROPAGATION AND CULTIVATION
SEEDS

- To propagate by seed, first collect the capsules when they are browning and splitting along the stems.
- Keep the capsules dry in a paper bag until you separate the seeds.
- Crack open the capsules by hand or using a hammer, while being careful not to damage the seeds inside.
- Wash off the sticky white latex from the seeds with soap in a strainer under running water.
- Best to start seeds fresh, soak the seeds in tap water for twenty-four hours; or do not use any pretreatment, as they will still germinate in three to nine months.
- Sow the seeds into a mix of 3 parts perlite to 1 part potting mix (3:1) then cover the seeds with ½ inch of mix.
- Keep them in a shaded, covered area and water every other day.

GERMINATION (SLOW-GROWING)

- Germination of seeds can take from three to nine months for all viable seeds to sprout. Some species take longer than others.
- Wait until four to six true leaves develop before transplanting them into a well-draining mix.
- Use 2-4-inch pots, water in the seedlings and then water weekly; foliar feed them monthly.
- Keep the seedlings in a shaded area; repot them into larger pots in five to six months.
- Move them into partial to full sun to harden them off and prepare them for outplanting.

CUTTINGS

- Choose the leafy semi-hardwood cuttings that have partially matured and taken after the spring flush of growth; follow the protocols provided for semi-hardwood cuttings.
- Use a mix of 3 parts perlite to 1 part potting mix (3:1) in a shallow flat; treat the base of the cuttings with rooting powder No. 1 or Rootone® No. 3, which has a fungicide in it.
- For these cuttings it is best to put them in a mist system (scheduled from 6 AM to 6 PM).
- The cuttings should develop roots in three to five months; when they do, transplant and care for them the same as for your seedlings.

OUTPLANTING

- Your hō'awa will be ready for outplanting in one to two years or when they have outgrown a 1–2-gallon pot.
- Choose a site similar to the environment the seeds and cuttings were collected in; for instance, do not plant a wet forest species in a dry forest habitat.
- Amend the soil to be well-draining; also mix in small amounts of 8-8-8 NPK fertilizer.
- Plant with other plants such as ferns and ground covers; allow for plenty of room for your hō'awa to grow to their full potential.
- Water in your plants and then water weekly; monitor the soil for moisture level and water when it is dry until the plants are well established, indicated by new foliar growth.
- Add small amounts of 8-8-8 or 14-14-14 NPK fertilizer every four to six months.

PESTS

- Ants living at the base of hō'awa will weaken the roots, and they will farm mealybugs, aphids (which transmit viruses to your plant), and scales; control the insects with natural horticultural oils and use bait for the ants.
- Red spider mites are tiny red mites that live on the underside of leaves, sucking out the chlorophyll and causing the leaves to yellow and fall off with time. Spray under the leaves with water when watering, or rotate spray with horticultural oils (neem or mitecides).

'Ilima

(Mallow Family)

HAWAIIAN NAME:
'Ilima

GENUS:
Sida

Full Sun

Range: Hawaiian Indigenous

Description: ground cover to shrub

Propagation: seeds

Sida fallax, 'ilima papa — CC

GENERAL DESCRIPTION

'Ilima grow as low, prostrate shrubs or small, erect shrubs up to 4 feet in height. They occur on dry coastal to diverse mesic forests up to 2,000 feet elevation. 'Ilima is by far the simplest genus of this family to grow and maintain in drier landscapes. Plants that grow in coastal habitats have lower growth habits and smaller, grayer leaves to reflect the harsh sun and tolerate the ocean spray. The double flower varieties are strung into leis (the lei of O'ahu), and come in an array of colors from yellow to dull red. The blossoms can be 1 inch across, and develops near the branch tips. Small brown, star-shaped capsules contain about five tiny fuzzy brown seeds that germinate easily becoming weedy in your garden, which is a good thing. 'Ilima does not root into the ground from its nodes like the *Jacquemontia*. The two species make great companions in the garden as ground covers. Hawaiians used the flowers and roots medicinally (Neal 1965).

'Ilima flowers — F&KS

Entire Range: Indigenous to Midway Atoll, Nihoa, and all main Hawaiian Islands.

Wild Habitat: Coastal dry habitats

Habit: Prostrate spreading to erect branching shrub

Mature Height: Ground level to 4 feet (1.2 m) in height

Stem/Trunk: Stems herbaceous, semi-woody to woody, smooth to fuzzy (covered with hairs)

Leaves: Leaves simple, heart-shaped, usually unlobed, margins with teeth, smooth or velvety and silvery due to covering of hairs, short leaf stalks, and stipules present

Inflorescence/Flower: Solitary, emerging from leaf axils or at the branch ends, golden yellow to orange-yellow, flower parts in multiples of five, and staminal column yellow

Fruit: Fruit a schizocarp, star-shaped, with six to nine locular chambers (mericarp) pale brown to black, about 3–4 mm long

Seed: Seeds brown or black, 1–2 mm long (Wagner et al. 1990)

PROPAGATION AND CULTIVATION SEEDS

- To propagate from seeds, first collect the mature dry star-shaped capsules; keep them dry in a paper bag until cleaned.
- Separate the seeds from the capsules as recommended for small dry seeds.
- The seeds can be stored using any of the methods discussed.
- Soak the seeds in hand-hot or tap water for twenty-four hours.
- Surface sow on dry media of 3 parts perlite to 1 part potting mix (3:1) in a shallow flat; water the seeds in.
- Keep them in a covered area to protect them from too much moisture.

GERMINATION

- Your ʻilima will germinate in about two weeks to two months for all viable seeds to sprout.
- Wait until the seedlings have two to four true leaves before transplanting into 2–4 inch pots.
- Use a well-draining mix with small amounts of 8-8-8 NPK fertilizer.
- Repot into larger pots and add new media every two to three months (fast-growing).
- Foliar feed them monthly; keep them more on the dry side.
- Move them into full sun to harden them off and prepare them for out-planting.

OUTPLANTING

- Your ʻilima will be ready to outplant when they have outgrown a 4–6-inch pot, which can take about six months.
- Choose a site with well-draining soil; it can be cindery or sandy, and it should be in full sun.
- Water your plants in, and then only water in times of prolonged drought.
- Foliar feed your ʻilima monthly on average for healthier growth.
- An ideal planting can be done by creating a cinder mound with the contrasting ʻilimaʼs gray foliage and yellow flowers; this makes a very attractive landscape.
- Plants can tolerate trimming if needed.

PESTS

- Ants and their associated pests (scales, mealybugs, and aphids) can infest your ʻilima plants and become terrible pests; use a systemic pesticide and control them according to the protocols for ants.
- Red spider mites can take up residence on the underside of the leaves. If they do, spray your plants with horticultural oil.
- Rust spots or small raised orange spots can appear on the underside of the leaves if the plant receives too much shade and moisture. To treat, reduce both moisture and shade.

Koa

(Legume or Pea Family)

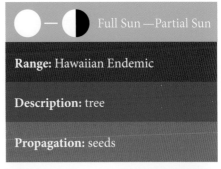

○ — ◑ Full Sun — Partial Sun

Range: Hawaiian Endemic

Description: tree

Propagation: seeds

HAWAIIAN NAMES:
Koa; Koaiʻa; Koaiʻe; Koaʻohā

GENUS:
Acacia

Koa tree — KL

GENERAL DESCRIPTION

Koa is the second most dominant tree of the upper dry to wet forests of Hawaiʻi (ʻŌhiʻa being the first). Koa is easily recognized by its 50–115 feet stature and spreading branches. What look like gray-green sickle-shaped leaves are really modified leaf stalks or phyllodes. The seedlings and juvenile trees also can have finely divided darker green compound leaves, which change into phyllodes with maturity. The lemon yellow flowers are small puffs forming near the branch ends, as do the flat thin pods that turn brown when fully developed. Each pod contains six to ten shiny flat black seeds. These are often eaten by seed weevils that feed on the embryos making the seeds nonviable. Recently in my yard, I have observed introduced rose-ringed parakeets eating the seeds through the pods. The two different native species can be identified by a combination of characteristics but the most obvious one is how their seeds are arranged in the pods. If they are horizontally arranged it is *A. koa* and if the seeds are arranged vertically, it is *A. koaia.*

One of the many things I like, in addition to the beauty of the koa, is the aroma from the nitrogen-fixing fungus associated with the roots. You may notice it when digging near a plant or when you are planting a seedling because it comes from the roots and the surrounding soils. Even the seeds and tiny seedlings have this odor when handled. The highly prized koa wood is reddish-brown with lighter tan streaks. It is used for traditional crafts, lumber, and woodworking. These trees are used in reforestation and it has great potential for further use in the commercial landscape industry in the Hawaiian Islands and possibly other tropical regions. A myth that I often hear is that koa cannot grow at the lower elevations. I have healthy *A. koa* and *A. koaia* trees growing in my yard at 200-300 ft elevation and they are vigorous and do not demonstrate elevation problems. I have seen fungal root problems result from too much moisture in the soil.

Please give koa trees a chance in your landscaping. They are very striking trees with their gray-green sickle-shaped phyllodes. They tolerate heavy pruning so they can be kept smaller, and a big plus is that the koa tree adds nitrogen to the surrounding soil, improving soil quality and health.

Entire Range: Hawaiian endemic

Wild Habitat: Lowland to upper dry, mesic, and wet forests

Habit: Branching tree

Mature Height: 35 m

Stem/Trunk: Beautiful grained (reddish-brown with tan streaks, hardwood, bark grayish to brown; trunk can reach 1–2 m in diameter) in older trees

Leaves: Mature leaves are sickle-shaped phyllodes, which are modified leaf stalks, and pale grayish-green; new leaf growth is bi-pinnately compound leaves, green and of various sizes

Inflorescence/Flower: Flowers are perfect, about 2 mm long and mimosaceous (like a Mimosa). The corolla is cream colored, the stamens curled, and more than twice as long as the corolla. The flower heads are in axillary racemes, and sometimes congested into leafy terminal panicles. The ovary is superior and pubescent

Fruit: Flattened, oblong pods, sometimes with constrictions between seeds, and with straight sutures (8–30 cm long and 0.8–2.5 cm wide)

Seed: Seeds are ellipsoid, flattened laterally, about 10 mm long by 5 mm wide, and a dark brownish-black (Wagner et al. 1990)

PROPAGATION AND CULTIVATION

It is better to propagate large trees with wide-spreading canopies from seeds rather than from cuttings or air layers. Seedlings provide a stronger, healthier root system, allowing the tree to obtain better nutrition and more stabilization, especially during strong winds.

Koa flowers and seeds — KL

SEEDS (EASY)

- To propagate from seed, first collect the brown pods; remove the black seeds from pods as soon as possible to reduce insect damage from seed weevils.
- If insect damage is a problem, soak the seeds in water; discard the seeds that float as they are nonviable.
- The seeds can be stored in desiccation chambers, at room temperature, or in refrigeration for up to ten years.
- For the fastest and highest germination rates, scarify the seeds as recommended.
- For large numbers of seeds, soak in hand-hot or tap water for twenty-four hours. Not all of the seeds will swell (the swelled seeds will germinate first), and germination will occur between eight days to one year.
- Place the seeds flat and ¼ inch apart in a leveled mix of 3 parts perlite to 1 part potting mix (3:1), and then cover the seeds with ¼ inch of additional mix.
- Water the seeds in, then water every other day. Keep them in a covered area.

GERMINATION

- Germination may take from eight days to two months for all scarified seeds to sprout. It can take four to twelve months for all soaked seeds to germinate.
- Transplant the seedlings into 4-inch pots (or taproot pots) when two to four true leaves develop; use a well-draining mix.
- Keep the potted seedlings in a covered, shaded place for a few weeks, and then move them into more sun.
- Repot the plants into 1-gallon pots in four to six months; do not allow your trees to become root-bound in the pots at any time because this causes an unhealthy root system which may result in the early death of the tree.

Koa seedlings — KL

- Move the plants into full sun to harden them off before outplanting them.
- *A. koa* is a faster-growing, stronger tree than *A. koaia*. The health of the parent plant determines how healthy the seedlings will be.

OUTPLANTING
- Both koa and koaiʻa grow well at about 200 feet elevation. They are low-maintenance trees and attractive landscape components.
- The trees will be ready for outplanting in about one year, when they have outgrown a 1- to 2-gallon pot.
- Choose a site in full to partial sun, and if it is a windy area, provide support to the young trees until they become established and stable.
- Amend the planting hole as recommended for soil to be well-draining, and fertilize with a small amount of 8-8-8 or 10-10-10 NPK Fertilizer.
- If the plants have become root-bound, gently loosen the circling roots to avoid unhealthy growth. Try to straighten the roots out into the planting

hole. They will tolerate some root pruning (never remove more than half of the root mass).

- Water them weekly until they become established, then water only in times of prolonged drought.
- Koa can be pruned back to keep the size of the tree manageable in small spaces.
- A good companion for the koa tree is the native sandalwood.

PESTS
- Koa can attract many pests such as ants, scale, and red spider mites. If they become infested with these control them as directed.
- Black twig borers lay their eggs into the stem of the young plants, and then the larvae eat the pith, killing or damaging the young plants. If you discover black twig borers in your koa, cut off all affected parts. What remains of the plant will sometimes grow back, depending on the age of the plant. Also apply a systemic pesticide, following the directions on the label.
- Seed weevils and rose-ringed parakeets eat the seeds, rendering them nonviable in most cases.

Native Koa bug on leaves — F&KS

Koʻokoʻolau

(Sunflower Family)

HAWAIIAN NAMES:
Koʻokoʻolau; Koʻolau

GENUS:
Bidens

Sun Requirements: Species specific

Range: Hawaiian Endemic

Description: erect perennial or annual herb

Propagation: seeds and cuttings

Koʻokoʻolau flowers — F&KS

GENERAL DESCRIPTION

Erect short-lived perennial or annual herbs, very adaptable. The common weed *Bidens pilosa* (Spanish needle) probably looked much like its ancestor, whose fruit arrived hooked on the feathers of marine birds, but since then the native species have lost this dispersal mechanism. The seeds can spread and become weedy if outplanted in your yard, which is a good thing if you are using the leaves for tea. Koʻokoʻolau leaves are used in a healing tea for diabetes (Levon Ohai 2000).

Entire Range: Hawaiian endemic

Wild Habitat: Summit ridges, cliffs, mesic forests, diverse mesic forests, windward coasts, coastal bluffs and cliffs, slopes, subalpine woodland to wet forest, bogs, lithified sand dunes, shrubland and dry slopes, and disturbed areas

Habit: Adaptable erect perennial or annual herb

Mature Height: 0.3–13 ft (0.1–4.0 m)

Stem/Trunk: Erect, decumbent, scandent (climbing), or suffrutescent (a perennial plant that is somewhat woody at the base) annual or perennial herb

Leaves: Simple, serrate or pinnately to tripinnately compound, opposite, pubescent or glabrous

Inflorescence/Flower: Heads solitary on long peduncles or in simple to compound cymes terminating the main stem and lateral branches, or only on lateral branches, radiate or discoid; rays yellow, white, orange, or red; disk florets perfect or pistillate, corollas yellow or orange, five-lobed

Fruit: Achenes obovate (inversely egg-shaped)-oblong, cuneate (wedge-shaped), or linear, obcompressed, curved, twisted, or coiled, occasionally with lateral wings, setose (covered with bristles) or glabrous (without hairs or glands)

Seed: The seeds are small and dry (Wagner et al. 1990)

PROPAGATION AND CULTIVATION SEEDS (VERY EASY)

- To propagate by seed, first collect fruits (achenes) when dry and brownish-black, and keep them dry by storing them in a paper bag.
- Clean the dry seeds and separate them from debris; viable seeds have a slight thickness to them when squeezed between the fingers.
- No pretreatments are needed; surface sow the thin seeds in a leveled mix of 3 parts perlite to 1 part potting mix (3:1).
- Water the seeds in, and then water them every other day.
- Keep them in a protected, shaded area.

Bidens wiebkei seed heads — SP

GERMINATION (FAST)

- If the seeds are viable, wait one week to two months to allow all of them to sprout.
- Transplant them into 4-inch pots after four true leaves develop.
- These plants are fast growing; keep them in the shade for two weeks, then move them to partial shade to full sun to help them acclimate.

CUTTINGS (EASY)

- Collect softwood tip cuttings 3–4 inches long, with at least three nodes, in the morning hours. It is best if they are taken in the spring or summer months. If plants are stressed or flowering, they will have a lower rooting percentage.
- Remove the lower foliage and cut the top foliage in half, to reduce moisture loss.
- Start cuttings as soon as possible, or store them in the refrigerator in a sealed plastic bag to hold in the moisture.
- Keep the cuttings moist at all times and out of full sun.
- Use a shallow flat of 3 parts perlite to 1 part potting mix (3:1) or 3 parts perlite to 1 part vermiculite (3:1).
- No rooting powders are necessary; insert at least one of the bottom nodes into the potting mix.
- Water the cuttings in, and then water them every other day.
- Keep them in a shaded, covered area.
- Cuttings will root in about two months. Once rooted, carefully remove them and repot into 4-inch pots.
- Water them in, keep them in the shade for two weeks, and then move them to more sun.

OUTPLANTING

- Your cuttings and seedlings may be ready for outplanting in four to six months.
- Choose a site in full to filtered sun (species specific), and out of strong wind.
- Amend the planting holes as recommended for good drainage.
- Some of the more common species can become weedy in a landscape setting, which is a good thing if you're using the leaves for tea.

PESTS

- Pests may include red spider mites, which hide on the undersides of leaves, causing leaf yellowing. To control them, apply a spray of horticultural oil.
- Ants, mealybugs, and scales can also attack *Bidens*. Treat them with the recommended ant bait and a scale and mealybug pest control.

Kou

(Borage Family)

HAWAIIAN NAME:
Kou

GENUS:
Cordia

○ Full Sun

Range: Indigenous

Description: tree

Propagation: seeds

Kou flowers — KL

GENERAL DESCRIPTION:

Kou is a fast growing, easy to propagate tree, suitable for hot coastal landscapes. Used in ancient and in present times as an excellent shade tree with large evergreen leaves and a wide-spreading crown. Throughout the Pacific the orange scentless flowers are used in leis and are associated with many everlasting myths and legends and the seeds were regard as a famine food.

Kou's durable yet easily worked wood has been flawlessly carved into 'umeke la'au (wooden containers) for food and water, as well as house posts, outrigger canoes and other carved artifacts. Kou is known as one of the four best woods, koa, milo and kamani others for carving in Hawai'i (Abbott et al 1992).

Kou seeds were thought to be transported to Hawai'i by early Polynesians. It is now believed to be an indigenous species, as evidenced from sediments at Makauwahi Cave (Burney et al 2001). This evidence indicates that kou seeds arrived before man, probably by wave-flotation.

Range: Indigenous to Pacific Islands, in Hawaii on all main Hawaiian Islands except Kahoʻolawe.

Wild Habitat: Forming thickets, sometimes wide-spread in low elevation, dry, coastal areas.

Habit: Tall, erect trees 17-34 feet, 23 feet spread, readily producing shoots from extensive shallow roots. Trunk bark mottled pale gray to tan, grooved and flaky.

Leaves: leaves thin, coriaceous, broadly ovate to elliptic, blades 10-20cm long, 8-16cm wide, tomentose along the main veins on the lower surface, otherwise glabrous, margins entire to undulate, apex acuminate, base subcordate to rounded or acute, petioles 4-12 cm long.

Flowers/inflorescence: Flowers in open cymes; calyx pale green, glossy, ca 1cm long, the lobes ciliate; corolla orange 5-7 lobed, the tube darker than the lobes, 2.3-3cm long, the lobes wrinkled, 3-4.5cm long.

Fruit/seeds: Fruit green when young, becoming brown and dry at maturity, subglobose to broadly ovoid, sometimes slightly asymmetrical, 2-3cm long, surrounded by the enlarged persistent calyx, seeds 4, white, usually 1-1.3cm long. (Wagner et al. 1990)

PROPAGATION AND CULTIVATIONS SEEDS (EASY)

- To propagate by seed, first collect the brown fruits when mature and falling to the ground. Keep dry in a paper bag until sowing.
- Start the fruits fresh; soak them in water for 24 hours to hurry germination. They'll float (that is how they traveled to the islands). Let dry.
- Place the treated fruits in a shallow flat or 6 inch pot of 3 parts perlite to 1 part potting mix (3:1). Water them in.
- Keep the flat in a covered protected area. Water every other day or when dry.

Kou seedlings — KL

GERMINATION

- In a month or so, move the sprouting seedlings into an area with partial sun for healthy growth.
- The fruit contains four seeds which may sprout at the same time. Once each of the seedlings has two true leaves, gently separate each one.

- Transplant the seedlings into their own 4-inch pots with a well-draining mix. Poor drainage and too much moisture in the media will rot the roots.

C. subcordata seeds – Maui—F&KS

- Keep newly potted seedlings in the shade for a week or so, and then move them into full sun to harden them off.
- Water them when they are dry; fertilize with a foliar feed every month for vigorous growth.
- Repot them every three to five months into one gallon pots adding new media.

CUTTINGS

Not recommended for trees. Kou seeds grow fast and develop a healthier root system than cuttings.

OUTPLANTING

- Ready for outplanting when the tree has outgrown a 1-gallon pot in about six months to a year.
- Kou tend not to become root bound in the pots because of their fibrous root system. By comparison, a koa seedling easily becomes root bound in pots due to its fast growing tap roots.
- When preparing to outplant, choose a dry location in the full sun with well-draining soil and amend the soil as recommended.
- Water in the plants at first, then only water periodically when dry. If there is a water shortage, presoaked polymer granules can provide the temporary moisture needed.
- Fertilize your kou with 10-10-10 every six months or foliar feed monthly for faster growth.

PESTS

Mealybugs on the plant and in the roots can attack kou; baiting can control the ants and the mealybugs can be managed with a systemic pesticide.

Loulu

(Palm Family)

HAWAIIAN NAME:
Loulu

GENUS:
Pritchardia

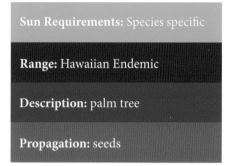

Sun Requirements: Species specific

Range: Hawaiian Endemic

Description: palm tree

Propagation: seeds

Pritchardia hillebrandii palms on Huelo rock, Moloka'i — KRW

Pritchardia kaalae – O'ahu — SP

GENERAL DESCRIPTION

Pritchardia is the only palm genus native to Hawai'i. They are monocots, solitary, unarmed medium to tall trees with fan-shaped leaves. Their flowers appear in an attractive inflorescence, which develops green fruit over several months, turning blackish when mature. *Pritchardia* are very attractive in the landscape; *P. hillebrandii* and *P. remota* will thrive in coastal plantings. I have found that sometimes the seedlings sprout as short-lived albinos, all white, living up to three months before dying from lack of chlorophyll. Five new species have been added to the list and four submerged with other species, *affinis, aymer-robinsonii, limahuliensis, lanaiensis*

Entire Range: Hawaiian endemic

Pritchardia hillebrandii – Huelo rock, Moloka'i — KRW *Pritchardia* sp. fruits – Maui — DR

Wild Habitat: Low land habitats to mesic diverse forests

Habit: Solitary, erect palm, unarmed, with a crown of palmate leaves

Mature Height: 30–120 ft (10–40 m)

Stem/Trunk: Solitary, longitudinally grooved, smooth, fibrous

Leaves: Costapalmate with petioles of various lengths

Inflorescence/Flower: Perfect flowers in multiples of three, pale white to yellowish, superior ovary, fragrant often attracting honeybees, borne on branching, complex, interfoliar inflorescences

Fruit: The fruits are a drupe, green and fibrous ripening to dark purplish-black

Seed: There is a single seed per fruit, hard endocarp and seed coat, with a white, homogenous, endosperm. (Wagner et al. 1990)

Pritchardia glabrata
flowers – Maui — KRW

PROPAGATION AND CULTIVATION SEEDS (EASY)

- It is important to wait until the fruit is ripe and turns brown to black in color before collecting. Fruits collected green usually are not fully developed, having thin seed coats (a covering,

Top to Bottom, Clockwise:
Pritchardia fruits soaking before removing pulp, NTBG nursery.
Cleaning palm seeds.
Cleaned palm seeds, NTBG nursery.
— All images by MC

that protects the embryo); these thin seeds coats will crack open during cleaning, exposing the fragile embryo to disease.

- Keep the pulp soft in a plastic bag; this also helps to ripen them.
- Remove the pulp by hand, or use a pocketknife.
- Soak the seeds either before or after cleaning for twenty-four hours in tap water, then air-dry them.
- Optional: soak in a weak bleach solution (1 tsp. of bleach to 1 gal. water) or fungicide (follow directions on label) for five to ten minutes; this helps to prevent fungal attack.
- Start palm seeds fresh. They do not store well, and lose their viability quickly when desiccated; however they can be refrigerated for a few months.
- The appropriate seed mix depends on where the palm has evolved. For wetter environments (needed by, for example, *P. waialealeana* and *P. vis-*

cosa) sow in moist sphagnum moss or cleaned black cinder and keep them in a mist system that is turned off at night.

- Use a potting mix made up of 3 parts perlite to 1 part potting mix (3:1), which works well for the other species; cover seeds with 1–2 inches of seed mix, depending on the seed size.
- Keep seed flats in a covered, shaded area, and water them every other day.
- Protect the seeds from rats by placing a wire screen over the flat, as they will try to find and eat the tasty endosperm.

Pritchardia limahuliensis seedlings – NTBG nursery — KL

GERMINATION

- Most loulu germinate in one to two months; seeds that were collected imm ture can take up to six months to sprout, if they sprout at all.
- Transplant as the seedlings germinate into 4 – 6-inch pots, to accommodate their stiff taproots.
- Choose a well-draining transplant mix, as recommended.
- Gently remove the seedlings by the leaves, not the roots, which are easily broken.
- The seed stays attached to the seedlings; bury all the roots up to the crown and seed.

Pritchardia viscose – NTBG nursery — KL

- Water them in, and keep the newly transplanted seedlings in a shaded area, elevated off the ground and away from toads (which like to nestle in the pots, displacing the seeds and seedlings) and other pests.
- In a few months move them into more sun to help harden them off for outplanting.
- Repot your palms into taller pots and new soil every six months or so, do not allow the roots to become thoroughly root-bound. Unhealthy roots make for an unhealthy plant in the long run; tall citrus pots work well for larger palms.

OUTPLANTING
- When the palm has outgrown a 2-gallon pot in two years or so, it is ready for outplanting.
- Amend the hole and soil as recommended. Loulu palms found in higher elevation do best in well-draining soils in partial shade; the lower elevation palms do better in full sun, and well-draining soil.

FERTILIZE
- Use a balanced fertilizer such as 8-8-8 NPK for transplanted seedlings
- Use 14-14-14 NPK for older plants one year and up.
- Apply every four to six months to keep the palm healthy; one indication of stress is the leaves yellowing.

PESTS
- Leafrollers are a native insect that cause holes and rips in the leaves as they eat; they then roll up in the leaves to pupate, not killing the palm, but making the plant look ragged. Use horticultural oil for control.
- Sugarcane borers will bore a hole in the side of the trunk of the palm and kill it as the grubs eat out the pith. The grubs will then pupate in the trunk, the palm may look healthy, but it can be dead within a week. Use a systemic pesticide (for example, a soil drench).
- Red spider mites on the underside of a leaf will cause the leaf to yellow; to treat, spray with a horticultural oil.
- Ants living at the base of the tree will farm a number of insects; control as recommended.
- Rats love to eat *Pritchardia* seeds, seedlings, and petioles (leaf stalk); look for claw marks and half-eaten seeds, or seedlings with their leaves gone; monocots have only one growing tip, which when removed will cause the plant to die. Set traps or cover the seed flats with small mesh wire.

Ma'o

(Mallow Family)

HAWAIIAN NAMES:
Ma'o; Huluhulu

COMMON NAME:
Hawaiian cotton

GENUS:
Gossypium

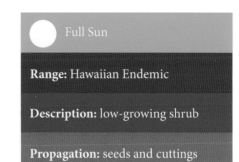

Full Sun

Range: Hawaiian Endemic

Description: low-growing shrub

Propagation: seeds and cuttings

Ma'o, Hawaiian cotton — F&KS

GENERAL DESCRIPTION

Ma'o is a low-growing shrub 2–6 inches high with attractive bright yellow solitary flowers (leaves used by the Hawaiians to make a light green dye (Abbott 1992)). They were once common in dry, rocky, coastal sites but are now vulnerable to the development of these seaside areas. The leaves are three to five lobed and are covered with a white down; they occur in dry areas with full sun. Medium-sized capsules contain two to four fuzzy seeds that are covered with short, brown, cotton fiber boles (which is not used commercially for cotton). Ma'o has been used as a hardy rootstock for grafting on hybrid cottons that produce superior cotton fibers; the ma'o is used for its disease and drought resistance. It is a great shrub for a coastal or dry forest planting. It is a handsome contrast when outplanted in a black cinder bed with its grayish leaves and bright yellow flowers. 'Ilima will enhance it even more if it is planted as a ground cover near by.

Entire Range: Hawaiian endemic

Wild Habitat: Arid, rocky, or clay coastal plains between sea level and 120 m elevation

Habit: Shrubs

Mature Height: 0.5–1.5 m tall

Stem/Trunk: Branching low woody shrub

Leaves: Leaves simple, pale green, heart-shaped with three to five palmate lobes; about 7 cm wide

Inflorescence/Flower: Solitary yellow flowers or a few on short cymes, three bracts, pedicel nectaries absent

Fruit: Three-celled capsules, leathery to woody, and about 1.5 cm long

Seed: Seeds about 5 mm long, covered with copious lint, reddish-brown in color (Wagner et al. 1990)

PROPAGATION AND CULTIVATION SEEDS (EASY)

- To propagate by seeds, first collect the capsules when they are dry, brown, and splitting along their seams; keep them dry in a paper bag.
- Remove the fuzzy seeds from the capsules by hand.
- The seeds can be stored in desiccation for up to six years, or kept dry at room temperature or in the refrigerator.
- Soak the seeds in tap water for twenty-four hours; the seeds will initially float because of the cotton fibers.
- Use a mix made up of 3 parts perlite to 1 part potting mix (3:1) in shallow flats; cover the seeds with an additional inch of mix.
- Water the seeds in and keep them in a covered area; water them twice a week or when it is dry.

GERMINATION

- Germination can take three weeks to two months for all viable seeds to sprout.
- When four to six true leaves develop, it is time to transplant them into 2-inch pots using a well-draining mix.
- A mix made up of 3 parts black cinder to 1 part potting mix (3:1) works well with a small amount of 8-8-8 NPK fertilizer added.

- Repot them when the plants are twice as tall as the pots they are growing in.
- Move them into full sun to help harden them off and prepare them for outplanting.

CUTTINGS
- Take semi-hardwood to softwood cuttings following the protocols described.
- Use a mix of 3 parts perlite to 1 part vermiculite (3:1) or 1 part potting mix (3:1), applying rooting powder Nos. 1–3.
- The cuttings should be rooted in two to three months.
- Once they have rooted, transplant and handle them the same as described for the seedlings.

OUTPLANTING
- Your maʻo will be ready for outplanting when they are twice as tall as the 4–6-inch pots, or in about six months.
- Choose a site in full sun with well-draining soil; amend the soil as recommended.
- Water them in, then water in times of drought; keep them on the dry side; no irrigation systems are necessary as fungal spots (powdery mildew) develop on the leaves if the plant site stays too moist.
- Foliar feed them monthly or apply 8-8-8 NPK fertilizer every six months.

PESTS
- Ants and pests they farm can infest your maʻo plants; use a systemic pesticide and control them according to the protocols for ants.
- Whiteflies can occur on the underside of the leaves; apply systemic pesticides or spray with horticultural oils.
- Red spider mites can take up residence on the underside of the leaves; if they do, spray your plants with horticultural oil.
- Powdery mildew (fungi) appears as a whitish powder on the leaves and spreads rapidly when the plants are kept wet from irrigation and over watering. Prune off the affected leaves and dispose of them to prevent the spread of the fungi. Reduce watering and spray the affected foliage with a fungicide following the directions on the manufacturer's label.

Maile

(Dogbane Family)

HAWAIIAN NAME:
Maile

GENUS:
Alyxia

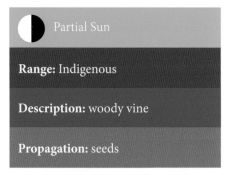

Partial Sun

Range: Indigenous

Description: woody vine

Propagation: seeds

Maile flowers — KJ

GENERAL DESCRIPTION

Maile is diverse both ecologically and morphologically. Usually, this liana (woody vine) twines or clambers up or over other plants in the wild. Its glossy leaves have variable shapes, depending on location. The small, yellow flowers mature into olive-shaped, purplish-black fruit. All parts of the plant contain coumarin, which emits a pleasant odor. Because of this, the maile was integrated into the Hawaiian culture as a very important and cherished plant, particularly for lei making. It can be grown easily as a backyard plant, making it readily accessible to the lei maker. My 20 year old maile vine climbed up and over native trees planted nearby, eventually killing them. Maile can become weedy if used in a landscape design. Keep trimmed or harvest for leis.

Entire Range: Indigenous to Hawai'i

Wild Habitat: Well adapted to a diversity of habitats including: dry open sites, mesic forests to closed wet forests

Habit: Twining liana (woody vine), scandent shrub, and sometimes a small erect shrub

Mature Height: 3–10 ft (1–3 m)

Stem/Trunk: Woody with milky sap

Leaves: Leaves variable, glossy above, paler below, glabrous (smooth, without hairs or glands), fragrant when crushed, margins entire, ternate (arranged in threes) or opposite, leaf shapes vary from lanceolate (lance-shaped) or ovate (egg-shaped) to linear-lanceolate, elliptic, or sub-orbicular (almost circular in outline)

Inflorescence/Flower: Flowers small, in axillary (arising from axil), umbellate cymes, peduncles (flower stalks) 1–1.5 cm long, corolla (petals) greenish to yellowish white

Fruit: Ovoid drupe, consisting of two to three one-seeded joints, ripening to dark purplish, pulpy fruit

Seed: One ovoid, furrowed seed per carpel (Wagner et al. 1990)

PROPAGATION AND CULTIVATION
SEEDS (EASY)

Maile seedlings — KL

- Alyxia is the easiest genus to propagate and grow within this family.
- Maile seeds have a high germination rate if the seeds are sown when fresh.
- It is important to collect the fruits (drupes) when they are mature, ripe, and the flesh is pulpy and purplish-black.
- Do not allow the pulp to dry around the seeds as this will reduce their viability. This can be prevented by keeping the fruits in a plastic bag to soften them. Alternatively, soak the seeds in water for an hour and clean off the pulp as directed.
- Start the seeds when they are fresh, with no pretreatments. Maile seeds do

not tolerate desiccation or storage, and they lose their viability as they dry out and age.
- Sow as directed for medium sized seeds, using 3 parts perlite or 3 parts fine black cinder to 1 part potting mix (3:1) in a shallow flat.
- Cover the seeds with ½ -inch layer of mix on top of the seeds.
- Keep them in a shaded, protected area and water them every other day. Do not let the mix dry out at any time.

GERMINATION
- Maile germinates over time; it may take it from one to six months for all viable seeds to sprout.
- Transplant the maile seedlings as they sprout and after they grow at least two true leaves. Note: it is important to handle the delicate seedlings only by the leaves or root-ball, and not by their very delicate long stems that can be easily injured.
- Maile do best in well-draining cinder soil or coarse perlite No. 3 used for added drainage within the potting mix.
- Keep the transplanted seedlings in a shaded area, and then gradually move them into an area with partial sun to harden them off for outplanting.
- Or they can be repotted into larger pots at this stage.

OUTPLANTING
- The maile will be ready for outplanting in six months to one year or when it has outgrown a 1-gallon pot.
- Provide something for the maile to grow upwards into or to grow over, such as a tree.
- Choose an area protected from strong winds. The area needs well-draining soil, or amend the site as directed. Add a small amount of 8-8-8 NPK fertilizer. Polymer can be used in areas that need help retaining soil moisture.
- Water them for the first month until the plants are established, then water only in times of drought.
- In tropical regions, it is best to plant maile during the rainy season.

PESTS
- Ants can be a pest of *Alyxia*. They set up camp at the base of the plant as they farm insects. Use the recommended ant treatment for control.
- Insects such as mealybugs or scales may occasionally be a problem. Control them as recommended.

Māmaki

(Nettle Family)

HAWAIIAN NAMES:
Māmaki, Māmake, Waimea

GENUS:
Pipturus

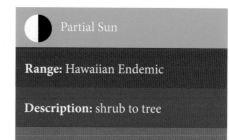

Māmaki — F&KS

GENERAL DESCRIPTION

Māmaki is a small tree up to 20 feet tall or a spreading shrub with watery sap and miniscule hairs along the branches. It has papery thin, alternate leaves that are tough and flexible. The flowers form in tight clusters at the leaf axils and have either male or female flower parts (unisexual), and both are found on the same plant (they sometimes occur as one sex per plant). The fruits are mulberry-like; the pulpy receptacles have many tiny brown seeds embedded throughout them. This genus was dispersed in the islands by birds, and it is said that the four endemic species are the result of a single colonizer (Wagner 1990). The Hawaiians made a coarse brown kapa and cordage from the fibrous bark; the whitish, pulpy fruits were eaten and used as a laxative, and the leaves were made into a tonic tea (Abbott 1992). The leaves of the māmaki are food for caterpillars of the native Kamehameha butterfly (*Vanessa tameamea*). In this family, the valuable māmaki is by far the easiest to grow from seeds and cuttings. This robust plant is also easy to maintain in the landscape if it is grown with the proper moisture and shade.

Entire Range: Hawaiian endemic

Wild Habitat: Mesic, diverse mesic to wet forests; subalpine to alpine regions

Habit: Shrubs to small trees

Mature Height: 1.5–6 m height

Stem/Trunk: Branches with watery sap and covered with fine or straight hairs

Leaves: Leaves are alternate, thin and papery to thicker and leathery, palmately veined, 3- to 5-nerved, veins are reddish and have concentrations of calcium carbonate along them which are visible on the upper surfaces; stipules

Inflorescence/Flower: Flowers are unisexual and occur in various combinations on different species; the minute flowers grow as clusters either sessile or in influences in the leaf axils

Fruit: The fruit has a pale-white, fleshy receptacle with the tiny achenes embedded in it

Seed: Small, dry seeds (Wagner et al. 1990)

PROPAGATION AND CULTIVATION SEEDS
- To propagate by seeds, first collect the whitish, pulpy fruits when soft and mature and keep them moist in a plastic bag until cleaned.
- Separate the tiny seeds from the pulp as directed for small pulpy seeds.
- Start the seeds fresh; no pretreatments are needed.
- Surface sow the seeds onto a mix of 3 parts perlite to 1 part potting mix (3:1), and water them in.
- Keep them in a shaded, covered area and water them every other day.
- Once the seedlings sprout, begin foliar feeding them monthly, using a light solution.

GERMINATION (HIGH RATE)
- All viable seeds from your māmaki will germinate in one to four months.
- Wait until four to six true leaves emerge, then carefully transplant them into 2-inch pots; be careful to avoid damaging the fine fibrous roots.

- Use a cindery mix for best results, and add in a small amount of 8-8-8 NPK fertilizer.
- Repot in two to four months, and move into partial shade.

CUTTINGS
- To clonally propagate by cuttings, first collect semi-hardwood tip cuttings from the top of the plant.
- Remove the lower leaves and keep the tips moist in a sealed plastic bag until you start them.
- Cut each stem into 5-inch pieces and cut the top foliage in half; apply rooting powder No. 1 to the recut stem bottoms.
- Insert at least one node into a moistened mix of 3 parts perlite to 1 part potting mix (3:1) and then water them in lightly, so as not to wash off the rooting powder.
- Keep the cuttings in an intermittent mist system to obtain the best results or in a shaded, covered area.
- They should be rooted in one to three months.
- Transplant the rooted cuttings into 3- to 4-inch pots with well-draining cindery mix.
- Keep the potted cutting moist in a shaded area, protected from drying winds.
- They grow fast and will need to be repotted in two to four months.

OUTPLANTING
- Your māmaki will be ready to plant out in about six months to one year, when they have outgrown a 1-gallon pot.
- Choose a site out of strong winds in partial shade with well-draining soil.
- Plant them with other plants, trees, and shrubs for added protection.
- Foliar feed them monthly and work a small amount of 8-8-8 NPK fertilizer into the soil every three to six months, depending on the rainfall and the health of the soil.
- Water them when it is dry until they are well established; monitor them closely for pests or poor drainage.

PESTS
- Ants and their associated pests (scales, mealybugs, thrips, and aphids) can infest your māmaki. These sucking insects will feed on the plant juices. Use a systemic pesticide to control them and bait for the ants according to the protocols for ants.
- I've had several māmaki in my yard at 300 feet elevation; they have not had any major pest problems.

Naio

(Myoporum Family)

HAWAIIAN NAMES:
Naio; Naeo; Naieo

COMMON NAME:
Bastard sandalwood

GENUS:
Myoporum

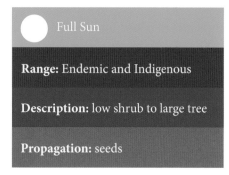

Full Sun

Range: Endemic and Indigenous

Description: low shrub to large tree

Propagation: seeds

Myoporum stellantum – O'ahu — SP

GENERAL DESCRIPTION

The naio grows as a many-branched, low shrub to large tree, depending on its habitat. It occurs most frequently in dry forests and growing near sea level. The leaves are alternate, 2–6 inches long, and dark green, clustering at branch ends. Flowers are small, pink to white, and five-parted. They cluster along the twigs, as do the small, rounded, whitish to purplish fruits that contain one corky, ribbed seed. The Hawaiians used the larger trunks and branches as hale (house) posts and smaller materials serve as thatching poles (Abbott 1992). It is called "bastard sandalwood" because of the strong hardwood, dark yellow-green and slight sandalwood scent. During the days of the sandalwood trade in the Hawaiian Islands, the naio was substituted for sandalwood when the prized wood was depleted from the forests. Naio is a very easy plant to grow and maintain in your garden and complements plantings of 'ilima *(Sida fallax)*, pā'ū-o-hi'iaka *(Jacquemontia ovalifolia)* or 'ākia *(Wikstroemia uva-ur-si)* grown underneath as ground covers.

Entire Range: Indigenous to Mangaia, Cook Islands, and all of the main Hawaiian Islands except Kaho'olawe

Wild Habitat: Strand vegetation, dry forest, lava, mesic to wet forest, subalpine forests, from sea level to 2,380 m

Habit: Shrub, branching small trees

Mature Height: 1–15 m height

Stem/Trunk: Stems erect to prostrate, smooth

Leaves: Leaves are simple, alternate, and variable in shape from elliptic to lance-shaped, about 15 cm long to about 3 cm wide, leaves can be fleshy, papery, and leathery, stipules absent. Leaves have entire margins, smooth surfaces; leaf stalks are about 2 cm long and are usually winged.

Inflorescence/Flower: Flowers perfect, irregular, axillary, usually between two and ten per cyme, calyx five-lobed, glandular, corolla white, and white with purplish-pink, bell-shaped

Fruit: Fruit a drupe, greenish-white to pinkish-purple, and ribbed when dry

Seed: Seeds spindle-shaped, one per cell, and papery when dry, about 2 mm long (Wagner et al. 1990)

PROPAGATION AND CULTIVATION SEEDS

- To propagate by seeds, first collect the fruits when they are soft and whitish or purplish in color, and keep them moist in a plastic bag.
- Separate the seeds from the pulp as recommended for medium pulpy seeds.
- Seeds can be stored for up to six years but are more viable when they are started fresh.
- Soak seeds in tap water for five days or in hand-hot water for thirty-six hours; the seeds will float at first, and then will sink if they are viable.
- Sow onto a leveled mix of 3 parts perlite to 1 part potting mix (3:1); then cover the seeds with ½ inch of additional mix, then water them in.

Myoporum sandwicense
seeds — F&KS

- Keep the flats in a covered area, moving into partial sun when the naio start to sprout. Do not allow the media to dry out at this time.
- Water every other day, foliar feed sprouted seedlings monthly.

GERMINATION

- Germination can take from one month for seeds soaked for five days, and up to six months for all other viable seeds to sprout.
- Wait until four to six true leaves develop, then transplant into 2–4-inch pots with well-draining mix and small amounts of 8-8-8 NPK fertilizer. Foliar feed them monthly.
- Repot them into larger pots and add new media every four to six months.
- Move into full sun to help prepare them for outplanting by hardening them off.

Myoporum sandwicense seedlings — PT

OUTPLANTING

- Your naio will be ready for outplanting in six months to a year, when they have outgrown a 1–2-gallon pot.
- Choose a site in full sun which is also out of direct strong winds; if the site is windy, provide support for the plants.
- Amend the planting hole and soil to create a well-draining site by adding cinder or other amendments as recommended in soil amendments.
- Water in your plants, then water monthly and monitor for proper drainage and moisture, watering in times of prolonged drought.
- Use small amounts of 8-8-8 or 14-14-14 NPK fertilizers, foliar feed your naio every couple of months.
- Naio are easy trees to maintain; they have little to no problems with adapting to different environments, providing the soil is well-draining.

PESTS

- Ants and their associated pests (scales, mealybugs, and aphids) can infest your naio plants; use a systemic pesticide and control them according to the protocols for ants.
- Poor drainage and damp soil will eventually kill this plant, which loves arid conditions.

Nehe

(Sunflower Family)

HAWAIIAN NAME:
Nehe

GENUS:
Lipochaeta / Melanthera

Sun —Shade
(differs for each species)

Range: Hawaiian Endemic

Description: ground cover to perennial herb (description differs for each species)

Propagation: seeds and cuttings

Lipochaeta succulenta flowers — DR

Melanthera tenuifolia flowers — SP

GENERAL DESCRIPTION

Hawaiian nehe occur as sprawling perennial herbs, slightly woody at the base. They root easily along the stems at the nodes, and the roots grow into the soil, holding it in place (some species are great ground covers). The light-green, simple leaves are opposite, large and thin, or tiny and thick, depending on the natural habitat. Nehe were a dominant part of the understory in certain coastal and mesic forests; half of the species are rare, extinct, or vulnerable because of habitat loss, browsing animals, and/or the many introduced plants that are more aggressive than nehe.

Entire Range: Hawaiian endemic

Wild Habitat: Pili grassland slopes, remnant dry forests, coastal and sea level, dry coastal and dry shrubland, diverse mesic forest, open areas and near lava flows, dry forest, and dry-mesic forest, locally moist dry forest, and disturbed areas

Habit: Somewhat woody perennial, rarely annual herbs

Mature Height: 8 inches to 16 ft (2–50 dm)

Stem/Trunk: With erect, spreading to prostrate stems, sometimes rooting at the nodes

Leaves: Simple, opposite, mostly smooth or pubescent, entire or pinnately lobed, rarely compound, petiolate, the petioles often winged, or sessile and the bases connate-perfoliate (stem appears to pass through the leaf)

Inflorescence/Flower: Solitary heads or in cymose clusters, terminal, radiate, rays yellow, entire to toothed, disk florets perfect and usually fertile, corollas yellow, 4- to 5-merous, pappus often of scales, often tipped with an awn

Fruit: Achenes smooth to sometimes winged, greatly enlarging at maturity

Seed: Small, dry seeds (Wagner et al. 1990)

PROPAGATION AND CULTIVATION SEEDS (EASY)

- To propagate by seeds, first collect the dry brown achenes in a paper bag, and keep them dry.
- Clean them as recommended for small dry seeds.
- Seeds can be stored in a desiccation chamber for up to six years, or refrigerated.
- No pretreatments are needed, surface sow the thin seeds, then water them in.
- Keep them in a covered, shaded area, and water them every other day.
- Germination
- It may take two weeks to two months for all of the viable seeds to germinate.
- Some of the endangered nehe have lower viability rates possibly from inbreeding.
- Transplant seedlings when they have at least four true leaves, in one to two months.
- Use a well-draining transplant mix, as recommended.
- Keep seedlings in the shade for one to two months, and then move them into more sun to help harden them off.

CUTTINGS

- Collect three-node softwood or green tip cuttings during the morning hours.

Nehe — F&KS

- Keep them moist in a sealed plastic bag.
- Remove all of the lower leaves and cut the top leaves in half.
- No rooting powders are necessary for herbs; make sure at least one node is buried under the mix.
- Use a mix of 3 parts perlite to 1 part potting mix (3:1) in a shallow flat, then water the cuttings in.
- Keep them in a shaded, covered area and water them every other day.
- If the cuttings dry out at any time before or during rooting, the survival rate is lowered.
- These cuttings will root in three months. At that time, gently remove the cuttings and pot them into 4-inch pots.
- Use the recommended transplant mix.

OUTPLANTING
- Your nehe will be ready for outplanting in six months or when the seedlings and cuttings have outgrown a 4-inch or 1-gallon pot.
- Accommodate the plant by mimicking its natural habitat (sunny and dry, or moist and shady) and your results will be better.
- All species need well-draining soil.
- Apply an 8-8-8 NPK fertilizer every six months.
- These plants like to be trimmed back when their growth gets unruly; you can utilize the trimmings to make new cuttings.

- The small leaf from of M. micrantha makes a nice hanging basket plant; to accomplish this use a mix made up of 2 or 3 parts potting mix to 1 part cinder (3:1).
- Drier species planted in moist, humid, or shady areas suffer from powdery mildew on the leaves (a whitish dust). (*L. succulenta*)
- Do not overplant an area. Allow for space between the plants, at least a foot.
- Water the ground, not the foliage. If the mildew gets out of hand, dust the plant with a sulfur-based fungicide.

PESTS

- Ants found at the base of the plant can be controlled as recommended.
- Ants can also farm scales and mealybugs; use the recommended ant protocol to keep them under control.

Nehe — F&KS

'Ōhi'a
(Myrtle Family)

HAWAIIAN NAMES:
'Ōhi'a; 'Ōhi'a Lehua; Lehua

GENUS:
Metrosideros

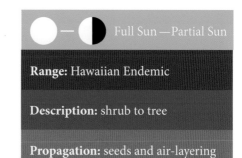

Full Sun—Partial Sun

Range: Hawaiian Endemic

Description: shrub to tree

Propagation: seeds and air-layering

'Ōhi'a Lehua — KL

GENERAL DESCRIPTION

There are many forms of 'ōhi'a; their seeds are wind dispersed, and the seedlings readily adapted to the many different habitats on the islands, from dry forests to bogs. Larger, rounded trees with smooth, oval-shaped leaves are found in wetter forests, whereas drier environments have produced smaller trees or shrubs with small, whitish hairy leaves to counteract the bright sun and dry conditions. Bog species are very small, only a few feet in height, and consist only of a few branches and sometimes even grow epiphytically on wet mossy logs. 'Ōhi'as are the most dominate tree in the Hawaiian forest and are genetically healthy because of their large and diverse populations. They hybridize easily, which results in many subspecies. Very tiny (dust-like) golden seeds develop in cup-like structures at the ends of the branches. They turn brown when they mature and they start to split open along their seams. Sometimes you can tell what color the flowers are going to be by the color of the

'Ōhi'a seeds — KL

seedling stems. For example, typically when seedlings are 1–2 inches tall, if they have pale yellow stems they will produce yellow flowers, and if they have red stems they will produce red flowers.

Rapid 'Ōhi'a Death/Ceratocystis Wilt of 'Ōhi'a: A newly identified disease has killed large numbers of mature 'ōhi'a trees (Metrosideros polymorpha) in forests and residential areas of the Puna and Hilo Districts of Hawai'i Island. Pathogenicity tests conducted by the USDA Agriculture Research Service have determined that the causal agent of the disease is the vascular wilt fungus, *Ceratocystis fimbriata* (Keith and others 2015). Although a different strain of *Ceratocystis fimbriata* has been present in Hawai'i as a pathogen of sweet potato for decades (Brown and Matsuura, 1941), this is a new strain of the fungus and the first record of any *Ceratocystis* species affecting 'ōhi'a. It is not yet known whether this widespread occurrence of 'ōhi'a mortality results from an introduction of an exotic strain of the fungus or whether this constitutes a new host of an existing strain. This disease has the potential to kill 'ōhi'a trees statewide. (Friday, 2015) UH-CTAHR.

To prevent further spread, do not transport any 'ōhi'a plant material to other islands or different districts on Hawai'i Island.

Entire Range: Hawaiian endemic to all of the main islands except Ni'ihau and Kaho'olawe

Wild Habitat: Bogs, dry, mesic, and wet forests

Habit: Stunted, prostrate shrubs, small trees to tall branching dominant forest trees

Mature Height: 0.1–30 m

Stem/Trunk: Bark fissured, light colored

Leaves: Leaves opposite, flattened (dorsiventral), size and shapes variable with species and habitats; some species or varieties have narrow lanceolate leaves, while others have obovate leaves

Inflorescence/Flower: Flowers red, orangish, and occasionally yellow; flower parts in multiples of five, flowers on pedicels, or occurring without a flower stalk, flowers borne from leaf axils, terminally or pedunculate inflorescences, or flowers solitary. Stamens numerous, extended twice as long as petals, giving the appearance of a "powder puff."

Fruit: Fruit a capsule

Seed: Seeds are narrow, linear, tiny, and numerous (Wagner et al. 1990)

PROPAGATION AND CULTIVATION SEEDS

- To propagate by seeds, first collect the capsules when they are brown, dry, and splitting open; keep them dry in a paper bag until cleaned.
- Separate the tiny seeds by opening the capsules by hand or as recommended for small dry seeds.
- The seeds can be stored in a desiccation chamber for no longer than three years, or refrigerated; germination results will be higher with freshly collected seeds.
- Seeds left at room temperature for a few months will also lose viability.
- Surface sow the tiny seeds onto a mix of 3 parts perlite to 1 part potting mix (3:1), or onto fine black cinder in a shallow flat 3 inches deep. Water the seeds in and keep them moist, then water every other day.
- Keep the flats in a shaded, covered area.
- Once the seedlings have germinated, foliar feed them monthly, using a weak solution.

'Ōhi'a seedlings — KL

'Ōhi'a lehua one-year-old seedling – NTBG — KL

GERMINATION

- Germination of all viable seeds can take from two weeks to three months.
- Very small seedlings need at least four true leaves (which can take about six months) before handling, and then only handle carefully by the leaves

'Ōhiʻa air layer — KL

or small root balls (not the delicate stems); follow the directions for transplanting.

- Transplant into 2-4-inch pots. Important: be sure that the mix is well-draining, use 3 parts black cinder to 1 part potting mix or other well-draining mix (3:1), adding small amounts of 8-8-8 NPK fertilizer.
- Keep the seedlings in a shaded area; repot them in four to six months, when they are twice as tall as their pots. The roots are very sensitive during this period; try not to disturb them at this time.
- Foliar feed them monthly, and move them into partial sun to harden them off and prepare them for outplanting.

AIR LAYERING (EASY)
- To make certain you get the 'ōhiʻa flower you desire, air layering is a guarantee
- Follow the directions for air layering; the air layers should be rooted in three to six months; use rooting powder Nos. 8–30, which all work.
- Do not attempt to air layer unless the bark is slipping (when it is removed from the stem easily)
- 'Ōhiʻa trees grown from seed have a healthier more established root system, making for stronger trees in the long run. Air layers which have younger

roots growing from the bark, need more care to survive outplanted.

OUTPLANTING
- Your ʻōhiʻa will be ready for outplanting in about two years when they are growing healthily and have outgrown a 2-gallon pot.
- Choose a site in partial to full sun, in well-draining soil, out of strong winds, and amend the ground as recommended. Plant with other plants like shrubs and ground covers.
- Poor soil drainage will eventually kill the ʻōhiʻa.
- Water them in, then monitor them weekly for moisture; water when it is dry, and in times of prolonged drought.
- Add small amounts of 8-8-8 NPK fertilizer every three to six months, and work the fertilizer into the soil.
- These are fairly easy plants to maintain in the landscape, with only a few problems; try to plant the ʻōhiʻa in a similar environment to where it was originally collected from for the best results.

PESTS
- Chinese rose beetle will eat holes in the leaves; apply a systemic pesticide as recommended.
- Ants and their associated pests (scales, mealybugs, and aphids) can infest your *Metrosideros* plants; use a systemic pesticide and control them according to the protocols for ants.
- Whiteflies might attack your ʻōhiʻa; when they do, wash them off with water by hand, or spray following the recommended directions.

Pāʻū-o-Hiʻiaka
(Morning Glory Family)

HAWAIIAN NAMES:
Pāʻū-o-Hiʻiaka; Kākua o Hiʻiaka

GENUS:
Jacquemontia

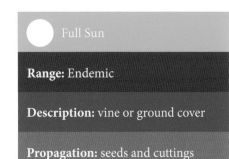

⬤ Full Sun	
Range: Endemic	
Description: vine or ground cover	
Propagation: seeds and cuttings	

J. sandwicensis flowers – Oʻahu — CC

GENERAL DESCRIPTION

Pāʻū-o-Hiʻiaka is a beautiful and easy plant to grow and maintain in a landscape. This sprawling vine is found in coastal areas throughout the islands. Often roots at the nodes to help hold the plant in place during strong coastal winds, with thick small, rounded leaves. *J. sandwicensis* from the drier southwest side of the Big island, their leaves are densely tomentose (white woolly hairs), giving the whole plant a silver appearance, which is very attractive, especially when planted with a black cinder background. The small pale blue flowers bloom from December through July, small dry tan seed capsules contain one to four roundish seeds. The leaves and stems of this plant were used by Hawaiians to treat babies with thrush (ʻea) and as a laxative (Wagner et al. 1990). It is a very attractive ground cover in drier gardens and stabilizes the soil by rooting at the nodes. It adds a great contrast when planted among low-growing ʻilima papa (*Sida fallax),* which does not root at the nodes.

Entire Range: *J. sandwicensis* is a Hawaiian endemic

Wild Habitat: Coastal strand habitats made up of various substrates

Habit: Herbaceous prostrate vine

Mature Height: 3 m long

Stem/Trunk: Stems are subglabrous to densely tomentose (hairy) with overlapping, two-branched hairs

Leaves: Leaves thick or fleshy, elliptic, 5 cm by 3 cm, entire margins

Inflorescence/Flower: Flowers in axillary cymes, with 5–10 mm pedicels (stalks), corolla pale blue or white, broadly campanulate (bell-shaped) 7–15 mm long

Fruit: Tan to brown capsules, quadrangular-globose, 4–6 mm in diameter, and enclosed by enlarged sepals

Seed: Seeds are one to four, trigonous (three-angled), 2–3 mm long, with or without winged margins; the seed coat is minutely areolate (marked by a different texture) and the seeds are sometimes faintly ruminate (Wagner et al. 1990)

PROPAGATION AND CULTIVATION SEEDS

- To propagate by seed, first collect the small capsules along the stem when they are dry and brownish-tan in color.
- Keep them dry in a paper bag until they can be cleaned.
- Separate the small brown seeds from the capsules as recommended for small dry seeds.
- No pretreatments are necessary; surface sow the seeds onto a dry mix with 3 parts perlite to 1 part potting mix (3:1) in a shallow pot or flat; water them in.
- Keep them in a protected, covered area.

GERMINATION

- Germination of all viable seeds may take one week to two months.
- Transplant them into 2-inch pots with a well-draining soil.
- Keep them in a shaded, protected area for two weeks; then move them into a site with full sun to harden them off.

CUTTINGS

- Take softwood cuttings in the morning hours from healthy plants.
- Remove all the foliage and the weak green tips of the cuttings, leaving 4–5 inch long pieces, each having at least three nodes.
- Keep them moist in a sealed plastic bag until you can pot them, no longer then a day or so.
- Use a shallow flat with a moistened mix of 3 parts perlite to 1 part vermiculite (3:1) and insert at least one node under the mix; no rooting powders are needed.
- Water the cuttings in; keep the flats in a covered, shaded area until rooted.
- Rooting in about two to three months; pot and care for them the same as for seedlings.

OUTPLANTING (FAST-GROWING)

- Pāʻū-o-Hiʻiaka will be ready for outplanting when they have outgrown a 4-inch to 6-inch pot, in about three months time.
- Choose a site in full sun with well-draining cindery or sandy soil.
- Give the vine room to spread and grow; outplant with low growing ʻilima as they grow well together, both liking the same dry environment.
- Water them in for two weeks and fertilize them with small amounts of 8-8-8 NPK fertilizer if they are growing slow and need a boost.

PESTS

- Ants can be pests; look for them at the base of the plant where they farm harmful insects such as mealybugs. They can be controlled using the recommended methods.
- Slugs can also be a nuisance; control them with the recommended slug bait.

Pāʻū o Hiʻiaka flowers — F&KS

Pōhinahina

Full Sun

(Verbena Family)

HAWAIIAN NAMES:
Pōhinahina; Pōlinalina; Kolokolo Kahakai

COMMON NAME:
Beach Vitex

GENUS:
Vitex

Range: Indigenous

Description: low branching shrub

Propagation: seeds and cuttings

V. rotundifolia flowers – Maui — F&KS

GENERAL DESCRIPTION

The hardy and attractive beach vitex occurs in the wild on sandy beaches. It grows as a low, trailing shrub with long, wide-spreading main stems that trail above or in the ground (sand) and roots readily at the nodes. The rounded gray-green leaves are opposite and silvery white on the underside, with many miniscule hairs that reflect the harsh sun and salt spray. Small clusters of purplish flowers develop at the branch tips. These ripen into the small, round, green fruit that blackens with maturity. The fruits have a corky layer typical of coastal plants. Pōhinahina make great coastal ground covers holding the dirt or sand in place with minimal maintenance. I have some in my yard, which is somewhat rainy at 300 feet elevation; the plants are doing great. They are planted in well-draining soil and only get partial sun. Vitex can handle heavy pruning; you can easily root the clippings instead of throwing them away.

Entire Range: Indigenous to China, Taiwan, Japan south to Malaysia, India, Sri Lanka, Mauritius, Australia, Pacific Islands, and Hawai'i: all of the main islands except Kaho'olawe

Wild Habitat: Strand plant, sandy beaches, rocky shores, and dunes

Habit: Low branching shrub

Mature Height: 1–3 dm height

Stem/Trunk: The stems root at the nodes, trail on the ground, form mats; side branches grow upright, and the branches are square in cross section

Leaves: Leaves are simple, opposite, compound with two to three leaflets, each leaflet roundish, the upper surface pale green, covered with a dense layer of fine hairs; lower leaf surface grayish-green; leaflet margins entire, leaf stalks about 1 cm long; the leaves have a sage-like odor and are aromatic when crushed

Inflorescence/Flower: Flowers are perfect, in short dense cymes, with minute bracts, bell-shaped calyx, blue-violet corolla, shaped like a funnel or trumpet and bilaterally symmetrical, with four smaller petals fused together until they reach the open end, and a bottom "lip" that is a bigger petal; five petals, four stamens in two pairs, extending beyond the flower opening; style extended beyond flower petals

Fruit: Fruit is a round drupe with a hard endocarp (layer surrounding the seed coat); green ripening to a dark bluish-black when ripe, about 6 mm in diameter

Seed: Seeds lack endosperm, and are roundish to oblong (Wagner et al. 1990)

PROPAGATION AND CULTIVATION SEEDS
- To propagate by seed, first collect the round, blackish fruit and keep them moist in a plastic bag until they are cleaned.
- Remove the thin, dark coat by massaging them against a wire strainer wall.
- Start the seeds fresh for higher germination rates.
- To pretreat the seeds, soak them in hand-hot or tap water for twenty-four hours. Note: the viable seeds are corky and tend to float.
- Sow the seeds onto a mix of 3 parts perlite to 1 part potting mix (3:1) then cover the seeds with an additional ½-inch of mix, and water them in.
- Keep them in a covered area, and water them every other day.
- Once the seedlings sprout, water them only when they are dry, but do not allow them to dry out completely.
-

GERMINATION
- All of the viable pōhinahina seeds will germinate in one to six months; germination is staggered, so wait a while before tossing out your seedling tray.
- These seedlings are slow-growing; wait until four true leaves form before transplanting them into 2-inch pots.
- Use a well-draining mix amended with 2 parts perlite or 2 parts fine black

cinder to 1 part potting mix (2:1).

- Keep them in the shade for two weeks, and then move them into full sun.
- Repot into larger pots every two to three months; the growth rate speeds up with age.

CUTTINGS (FASTER THAN SEEDS)

- To propagate clonally by cuttings, collect semi-hardwood cuttings that are 4–5-inches long from the main stems that root at the nodes along the ground.
- Remove and discard all of the thinner branches and leaves; keep them moist in a sealed plastic bag.
- Insert the recut bottom end of each stem into rooting powders No. 1 or 3, then into moistened mix made up of 3 parts perlite to 1 part vermiculite (3:1), lightly water the cuttings in, and be careful not to wash off the rooting powders.
- Keep them in a covered area, watering every other day.
- They should form roots in two to four months.
- When they are rooted, transplant them into 4-inch pots.
- Follow the handling and care directions given for the seedlings.

OUTPLANTING

- Your pōhinahina will be ready to plant out in six months to a year, when it has outgrown a 6-inch to 1-gallon pot.
- Choose a site with full sun and sandy or well-draining soil, amended as directed.
- Allow lots of room for the plant to spread out.
- Plant your pōhinahina with other shrubs such as ʻaʻaliʻi, and trees like wiliwili or naio.
- Water them in initially and then only water during prolonged periods of drought.

PESTS

- Spittle bugs may infest your plants. If they do, wash them off by hand, or spray them with rubbing alcohol.
- Ants and their associated pests (scales, mealybugs, thrips, and aphids) can infest your *Vitex;* these sucking insects will feed on the plant juices. Use a systemic pesticide to control them and bait for the ants according to the protocols for ants.

'Uki'uki

(Lily Family)

Full Sun — Partial Sun

HAWAIIAN NAMES:
'Uki'uki; 'Uki

GENUS:
Dianella

Range: Indigenous

Description: clumping perennial herb

Propagation: seeds

Dianella sandwicensis fruit — DB

GENERAL DESCRIPTION

'Uki is a common clumping perennial herb occurring in many habitats in the undergrowth with long, leathery, sword-shaped leaves 1–3 feet long, and 1 inch wide. These leaves were braided by the Hawaiians for cordage and used in house construction. Small, bluish-white flowers form on soft spikes that hang among the leaves. The bright blue fruits are eaten and dispersed by birds. The Hawaiians strung them into beautiful seed leis and also used the blue fruit extract as a dye for kapa (Abbott 1992). This is an easy plant to grow from their small black seeds and is best outplanted as an understory planting with trees, shrubs, and ground covers.

Entire Range: Indigenous to Hawai'i and extending at least to the Marquesas

Wild Habitat: Open to shady sites, wet to mesic forest, dry shrubland, grass-
    lands, and on lava

Habit: Perennial herb, forming clumps from the stems

Mature Height: 5–20 dm tall

Stem/Trunk: 'Uki has rhizomes which spread close to the ground and are about 1.5 cm in diameter

Leaves: Tough, flexible leaves, linear-lanceolate, smooth and green, 30–100 cm long and about 2–3 cm wide with a prominent keeled midrib and entire margins

Inflorescence/Flower: Blue to white perfect flowers with yellow stamens, flower parts in multiples of three occurring on panicles about 30 cm long and branching

Fruit: Deep blue berries, round and about 8 mm long

Seed: Seeds black, angular, and about 3 mm long with a brittle but hard seed coat (Wagner et al. 1990)

PROPAGATION AND CULTIVATION SEEDS

- To propagate by seeds, first collect the mature fruit when it is soft and dark blue in color; keep the fruit moist in a plastic bag.
- Separate the small black seeds from the purple pulp as directed for small pulpy seeds.
- Start the seeds fresh; no pretreatments are necessary, sow on a mix of 3 parts perlite to 1 part potting mix (3:1); add ½ inch of additional mix on

'Uki'uki seedlings – KL

top of the seeds.

- Water the seeds in, then water every one to two days and do not let the mix dry out.
- Keep them in a covered, shaded area.

GERMINATION

- It may take two to four months for all viable seeds to sprout.
- Wait until at least four leaves develop before transplanting into 2-inch pots filled with a well-draining mix.
- Water them in, and keep them in the shade.
- Repot every four months into larger pots or when they have grown twice as tall as their pots.

Dianella sandwicensis flowers — F&KS

- Foliar feed them monthly, or apply small amounts of 8-8-8 NPK fertilizer every six months.

OUTPLANTING

- Your plants will be ready for outplanting in about six to eight months, when they have outgrown a 6-inch or 1-gallon pot.
- Choose a site with partial to full sun and with well-draining soil. Amend the soil as directed.
- Water in the plants, then water weekly until they become established, which is indicated by new growth. Continue to fertilize with foliar fertilizer, and/or apply a slow-release 8-8-8 NPK fertilizer.

PESTS

Ants and their associated pests can infest your plants in the pots or at the base of the 'uki; if they do, apply a systemic pesticide and control them as recommended.

ʻŪlei

(Rose Family)

HAWAIIAN NAMES:
ʻŪlei; Eluehe; Uʻulei

GENUS:
Osteomeles

Full Sun — Partial Sun

Range: Indigenous

Description: small tree to ground cover

Propagation: seeds and cuttings

Osteomeles anthyllidifolia flowers — DR

GENERAL DESCRIPTION

ʻŪlei grows as a small evergreen tree 14 feet in height at higher elevations, to a low sprawling ground cover 1–2 feet high at sea level. The dark-green compound leaves are silvery underneath and covered with tiny hairs. Small, white, five-petaled flowers are slightly fragrant and cluster at the tips of the new growth. The round pulpy fruits are whitish-purple and contain four or five tan, wedge-shaped, stone-hard seeds. The seeds need to be soaked in water to speed up germination. Hawaiians used the long flexible stems to make scoop net handles. They used the flowers and fruits for lei pua, and the tough wood was used to make fishing spears and musical instruments (Abbott 1992). This is an easy plant to grow from seeds and cuttings, and requires little to no maintenance.

Entire Range: Indigenous to the Cook Islands, Tonga, and Hawaiʻi, on all of the main islands except Niʻihau and Kahoʻolawe

Wild Habitat: Found in a wide variety of habitats including coastal cliffs, dry to mesic forests, and disturbed areas

Habit: Erect to prostrate woody shrub

Mature Height: Up to 3 m in height

Stem/Trunk: Many-branched; the younger branches are grayish and drooping

Leaves: Leaves are leathery, compound with about twenty to twenty-five leaflets, with entire margins, glossy upper leaflet surface, prominent raised veins, some hairs along the midrib, underside of leaflets covered with hairs; brownish stipules

Inflorescence/Flower: Flowers in cymes that occur in terminal inflorescences, flower parts in multiples of five, with five whiter petals, five calyx lobes, fifteen to twenty stamens, and five styles; ovary is inferior

Fruit: The fruit of ʻūlei is a pome, white, fleshy, roundish, and about 1 cm in diameter

Seed: The seeds are yellowish and about 1.5 mm in diameter (Wagner et al. 1990)

PROPAGATION AND CULTIVATION SEEDS

- To propagate by seed, first collect the pulpy fruits when they are soft and whitish in color; keep them moist in a plastic bag.
- Separate the seeds from the pulp as recommended for pulpy seeds.
- Start the seeds fresh for best results, or store them cleaned and dried in refrigeration.
- Soak the seeds in hand-hot or tap water for twenty-four hours.
- After soaking, sow them onto a mix of 3 parts perlite to 1 part potting mix (3:1).
- Cover the seed with ½ inch of mix, and then water them in.
- Keep the flats in a covered, shaded area.

ʻŪlei seeds — KL

GERMINATION

- Germination of all viable seeds will take one to four months.
- Wait another month until two to four true leaves develop; then they will be ready to transplant into 2-4-inch pots.
- Keep them in partial sun and foliar feed them monthly.
- Repot them after three to five months, or when they have become twice as tall as their pots.

Osteomeles anthyllidifolia seedlings – NTBG nursery — KL

- Move them into full sun to help harden them off and prepare them for outplanting.
- Cuttings
- To clonally propagate your ʻūlei, first collect softwood to semi-hardwood cuttings in the spring or early summer when the plant is not in bloom and it is not seeding; follow the protocols for softwood and semi-hardwood cuttings.
- Apply rooting powder Nos. 1–3 at the stem base ends.
- Your cuttings should develop roots in three to five months. Cuttings taken in off-season (fall to winter) will root poorly if they root at all.
- Care for the cuttings the same as directed for the seedlings.

OUTPLANTING

- Your plants will be ready for outplanting in about six months to a year, when they have outgrown a 6-inch or 1-gallon pot.
- Choose a site in the full to partial sun with well-draining soil; amend the soil as directed.
- Water them in, then water weekly and when it is dry until the roots are established.
- Foliar feed them monthly and add small amounts of 8-8-8 NPK fertilizer every three to six months depending on the rainfall. If the soil is healthy, these plants will do well without added fertilizers.

PESTS

Ants and their associated pests (scales, mealybugs and aphids) can infest your ʻūlei; these sucking insects will feed on the plant juices. Use a systemic pesticide to control them and bait for the ants according to the protocols for ants.

Wiliwili

(Legume or Pea Family)

HAWAIIAN NAME:
Wiliwili

GENUS:
Erythrina

Full Sun

Range: Hawaiian Endemic

Description: tree

Propagation: seeds, cuttings, and air-layering

Erythrina sandwicensis flowers – Kaua'i — RY

GENERAL DESCRIPTION

Wiliwili is a large, dry-forest tree, 18–45 feet tall, with thin yellowish-orange bark. The leaves fall off during flowering and prolonged drought to conserve water loss. Flowers form in clusters at the branch ends, ranging in color from peach to light green, very attractive trees when they are in full bloom. The hairy brown pods are twisted when mature, giving the wiliwili (Hawaiian for "twist-twist") its name. Hawaiians used the soft, whitish wood for floatation purposes (such as surfboards, net floats, and for the outriggers on canoes). This is a very fast and easy to grow tree, which does well in dry lower elevations. The bright red-orange to purple bean-shaped seeds are used for making leis and are enjoyed by hungry rats and beetles.

Entire Range: Hawaiian endemic

Wild Habitat: Dry forest from sea level up to 600 m

Habit: Sparsely branching tree

Mature Height: 5–15 m

Stem/Trunk: The trunk has yellowish-orange bark, which is papery, with shallow fissures; the trunk and branches are sparsely armed

Erythrina sandwicensis seeds — CC

Leaves: The leaves are deciduous, pinnately trifoliate (leaflets in threes); leaves are obtuse to rounded with the terminal leaf almost triangular. Leaflets about 6 cm long by 7 cm wide. The leaflet upper surfaces are smooth, the undersides are tomentose (hairy); lateral leaf stalks about 5 mm long, the terminal leaf stalk about 15 cm long

Inflorescence/Flower: The flowers are papilionaceous (referring to a subfamily in the Fabaceae family named after the word root for "butterfly" because the flower resembles a butterfly and has an upper petal overlapping the others while in bud, two lateral wing petals, two keel petals, and ten stamens). The flowers are bilaterally symmetrical, perfect, and occur in terminal inflorescences. The corolla can vary from orange, yellow, white, to pale green

Fruit: The hanging pods are slightly woody and somewhat constricted between the seeds; they usually have one to three seeds per pod

Seed: The seeds are persistent, bean-like and are a showy red-orange to yellowish-orange, about 1.5 cm long by 1 cm wide, with a black hilum (Wagner et al. 1990)

PROPAGATION AND CULTIVATION SEEDS (EASY)

- To propagate from seed, first collect the pods when they are dry and brown. Remove the seeds by hand as soon as possible to avoid seed weevil damage.
- The seeds can be stored in a desiccation chamber, at room temperature, or in refrigeration for up to ten years.
- Scarify these large reddish seeds for fast germination.
- The seeds can be soaked in water for twenty-four hours with varied germination rates.
- Place the treated seeds flat in individual 4-inch pots or all together in 6–8-

Erythrina sandwicensis seed pods – Maui — HB

inch pots.

- Keep the seed mix on the dry side, especially for wiliwili from Kahoʻolawe, which should be sown in 100 percent perlite. For the wiliwili from other origins, sow in a mix of 3 parts perlite to 1 part potting mix (3:1) with an additional inch of mix on top of the seeds.
- Keep them in a covered area to control the moisture and water them weekly.
- Move the seedlings into an area with partial sun as they germinate.

GERMINATION (HIGH GERMINATION RATES)

- Germination can occur as soon as five days for pretreated seeds and up to a year for untreated seeds. Once they germinate, transplant them into tall 5-inch or taproot pots using a well-draining mix, poor drainage and too much moisture in the media will rot the roots.
- If the trees become root-bound, it will cause unhealthy root growth. Try to avoid this by repotting in a timely manner, and outplanting also in a timely way.
- Keep newly potted seedlings in the shade for a week or so, and then move them into full sun to harden them off.
- Water them when it is dry; fertilize with a foliar feed every month for healthy growth.
- Repot them every three to five months into taller pots and add new media.

CUTTINGS

- Take tip cuttings in the morning hours.
- Reduce all of the lower foliage, leaving only two to three leaves of new foliage at the tip.
- Make a 45° angle cut at the base and depending on cutting size apply rooting powders Nos. 8, 16, or 30 at the base end.
- Use a mix made of 3 parts perlite to 1 part vermiculite or 1 part fine black cinder (3:1).
- It may take about two to three months for the roots to develop.
- Once the roots have formed, transplant your cuttings into a cindery, well-draining mix.

Erythrina sandwicensis seedlings – NTBG nursery — KL

AIR LAYERING

- You can air layer the unwanted branches that you would normally throw away. Use lengths of 2–5 feet long, and ½–1 inch in diameter.
- Follow the directions for air layering and use rooting powders Nos. 16, 30, or 45 which all work well.
- The air layers will usually root in two to four months. Once they do, remove them from the tree and reduce their foliage by half. Pot up the air layers in tall, 1–3-gallon pots depending on size of the air layer.
- Use a well-draining soil mix so that the roots grow easily into the mix.
- Keep them in the shade and out of the wind for one month, then move them into an area with more sun, water only when dry, to keep roots from rotting.

OUTPLANTING

- The wiliwili will be ready for outplanting when the tree has outgrown a 1-gallon pot in about three to six months. It is a very fast-growing plant.
- When preparing to outplant choose a dry location in full sun with well-draining soil, and amend the soil as recommended.
- Water in the plants at first, then only water during times of prolonged drought. Do not water when the tree has lost its leaves; this is normal.
- Fertilize your trees with 8-8-8 or 10-10-10 NPK Fertilizer every six months or foliar feed monthly for faster growth.

PESTS

- Red spider mites can infest the wiliwili by occurring on the leaves, and ants may farm insects at the base of the plant. In each of these cases, control as directed.
- Mealybugs can infest the roots and stems. Use horticultural oils to control them.

Wiliwili – Maui —F&KS

- Powdery mildew can infest the leaves, especially if there is too much moisture. To manage this, first remove the affected leaves then reduce the frequency of watering.

Wiliwili pest eating leaves — KL

Photo Credits

GUIDE TO ABBREVIATIONS IDENTIFYING PHOTOGRAPHERS

HB	Heidi L. Bornhorst
DB	David S. Boynton
CC	Dr. Colleen Carroll
MC	Dr. Melany Chapin
KJ	Kathleen Johnson
KL	Kerin Lilleeng
DL	Dr. David H. Lorence
JO	John Obata
SP	Steve P. Perlman
DR	Dr. Diane Ragone
F&KS*	Forest and Kim Starr, USGS
PT	Dr. Peter Townsend
AW	Art Whistler
KRW	Ken R. Wood
RY	Randy Yokoyama

* I want to recognize Forest and Kim Starr for their valuable contribution to the conservation of Hawai'i's native ecosystems and their generosity with the many beautiful images they share with the public.

Bibliography

Abbott, I.A. *La'au Hawai'i: Traditional Hawaiian Uses of Plants*, 163. Honolulu: Bishop Museum Press, 1992.

Athens, J.S. and Ward, J.V. "Environmental Change and Prehistoric Polynesian Settlement in Hawai'i." In *Asian Perspectives*, 32(2): 205–223. Honolulu: University of Hawai'i Press, 1993.

Athens, J.S., Tuggle, H.D., Ward, J.V. and Welch, D.J. "Avifaunal Extinctions, Vegetation Change, and Polynesian Impacts in Prehistoric Hawai'i." In *Archaeological Oceania*, 37:57–78.

Burney, D.A., James, H.F., Burney, L.P., Olson, S.L., Kikuchi, W., Wagner, W.L., Burney, M., McCloskey, D., Kikuchi, D., Grady, F.V., Gage, R., and Nishek, R. "Fossil Evidence for a Diverse Biota from Kaua'i and Its Transformation Since Human Arrival." In *Ecological Monographs*, 71(4): 615–641. 2001.

Carquist, S. *Hawai'i, A Natural History*, 2nd edition, 468. Lawai: Pacific Tropical Botanical Garden, 1980.

Degener, O. *Plants of Hawai'i National Park, Illustrative of Plants and Customs of the South Seas*, 314. Ann Arbor: Edwards Brothers, Inc., 1945.

Grant, P.R. "Patterns on Islands and Microevolution." In *Evolution on Islands*, edited by Peter R. Grant, 1-17. New York: Oxford University Press, 1998.

Hartmann, H.T. and Kester, D.E. *Plant Propagation Principles and Practices*, 4th edition, 726. Upper Saddle River: Prentice-Hall, Inc., 1983.

Hawaiian Native and Naturalized Vascular Plants Checklist (December 2012 update) Editor: Clyde T. Imada, Hawaii Biological Survey Bishop Museum.

Hawaiian Vascular Plant Updates: Version 1.3 [12 April 2012], Warren L. Wagner, Derral R. Herbst, Nancy Khan, Tim Flynn

Judd, W.S., Campbell, C.S., Kellogg, E.A., and Stevens, P.F. *Plant Systematics: A Phylogenetic Approach*, 464. Sunderland: Sinauer Associates, Inc., 1999.

Lamb, S.H. *Native Trees and Shrubs of the Hawaiian Islands*, 160. Santa Fe: Sunstone Press, 1981.

McDonald, M.A. *Ka Lei the Leis of Hawaii*, 192. Kailua: Ku Pa'a Incorporated & Press Pacifica, 1989.

Neal, M.C. *In Gardens of Hawai'i*, 2nd edition, 924. Honolulu: Bishop Museum Press, 1965.

NTBG, National Tropical Botanical Garden, collection and research information.

Olkowski, W., Daar S., and Olkowski H. *Common-Sense Pest Control*, 715. Newtown: The Taunton Press, 1991.

Olson, S.L. and James, H.F. "Prodromus of the Fossil Avifauna of the Hawaiian Islands: Evidence for Wholesale Extinction by Man Before Western Contact." In *Science* 217:633–635. 1982.

Rauzon, M.J. *Isles of Refuge: Wildlife and History of the Northwestern Hawaiian Islands*, 205. Honolulu: University of Hawai'i Press, 2001.

Stokes, J.F.G. "Fish-poisoning in the Hawaiian Islands with Notes on the Custom in Southern Polynesia." In *Occasional Papers*, 7(10): 219–236. Honolulu: Bishop Museum Press, 1921.

Wagner, W.L., Herbst, D.R., and Sohmer, S.H. *Manual of the Flowering Plants of Hawai'i*, 1–2, 1853. Honolulu: Bishop Museum Press, 1990.

Wagner, W.L., Bruegmann, M.M., Herbst, D.M., and Lau, J.Q.C. "Hawaiian Vascular Plants at Risk." In *Occasional Papers, No. 60*, 58. Honolulu: Bishop Museum Press, 1999.

General Index

Hawaiian and Common Plant Names Index

Genera Index

About the Author

Kerin in her nursery 2005 — GR

Kerin Lilleeng immediately recognized the special nature of Hawai'i when she arrived in Hilo in 1968. Her fascination with Hawaiian plants, sparked by working with ti (Cordyline) cuttings, increased when she volunteered at the National Tropical Botanical Garden (NTBG) on Kaua'i. There, some of the finest horticultural experts taught her grafting, air layering, and other propagating methods and specialized horticultural techniques. Her natural green thumb and keen interest quickly earned her the position of being in charge of propagation for the NTBG volunteer plant site.

In 1988 Kerin volunteered for a community outreach program created at NTBG to increase public awareness by providing native Hawaiian plants to the community. She earned a reputation of being capable of growing "hard to grow" unknown plants.

A grant from the John D. and Catherine T. MacArthur Foundation was awarded to NTBG to create a resource center for understanding how to propagate native Hawaiian plants. The result of this grant, the Hawai'i Plant Conservation Center (HPCC), gave Kerin the opportunity to unlock the methods needed to propagate well over 800 species of native Hawaiian plants. She tried to mimic nature to figure out how to break dormancy, initiate germination, and successfully grow healthy seedlings and plants. Her work with the HPCC at NTBG provided much of the knowledge included in this book.

Kerin then took a position as research horticultural specialist with the Research Corporation of the University of Hawai'i (RCUH). Her work involved the cycle of collecting seeds, propagating them, and then planting them back out into their wild habitats. By experimenting with the plants at different elevations, Kerin increased her knowledge of what was possible when working with plants of various altitudes and vegetation regions.

Kerin has worked with the worldwide botanical community on various research efforts, has been the subject of several national and international articles on her unique knowledge, and has held classes for volunteers, the scientific community, specialists, and the general public. Today she is still considered to be the world leader in native Hawaiian plant propagation.

Her enthusiasm for sharing her knowledge of native plants with others has led to the publication of this book so that everyone and anyone can appreciate and enjoy growing the keiki o ka ʻāina (children of the land).

AWARDS:

Article: September 1997, United Airlines HEMISPHERES magazine Flower Power: Kerin Lilleeng-Rosenberger by Margaret A. Haapoja.

In March 11, 1998 in observance of Women's History Month, The Garden Club of Honolulu recognized me for my outstanding contribution to Horticulture and Conservation in Hawaiʻi.

2006 my book won the Ka Palapala Poʻokela Awards for Excellence in Natural Science from the Hawaiʻi Book Publishers Association.

Four-petaled kokiʻoʻula – KL